QUICKBOOKS

A Simple Guide to Quickly Learn Bookkeeping & Accounting for Beginners

By Joseph Tucker

© **Copyright 2021 - All rights reserved.**

The content contained within this book may not be reproduced, duplicated or transmitted without direct written permission from the author or the publisher.

Under no circumstances will any blame or legal responsibility be held against the publisher, or author, for any damages, reparation, or monetary loss due to the information contained within this book. Either directly or indirectly.

Legal Notice:

This book is copyright protected. This book is only for personal use. You cannot amend, distribute, sell, use, quote or paraphrase any part, or the content within this book, without the consent of the author or publisher.

Disclaimer Notice:

Please note the information contained within this document is for educational and entertainment purposes only. All effort has been executed to present accurate, up to date, and reliable, complete information. No warranties of any kind are declared or implied. Readers acknowledge that the author is not engaging in the rendering of legal, financial, medical or professional advice. The content within this book has been derived from various sources. Please consult a licensed professional before attempting any techniques outlined in this book.

By reading this document, the reader agrees that under no

circumstances is the author responsible for any losses, direct or indirect, which are incurred as a result of the use of information contained within this document, including, but not limited to, — errors, omissions, or inaccuracies.

Table of Contents

INTRODUCTION

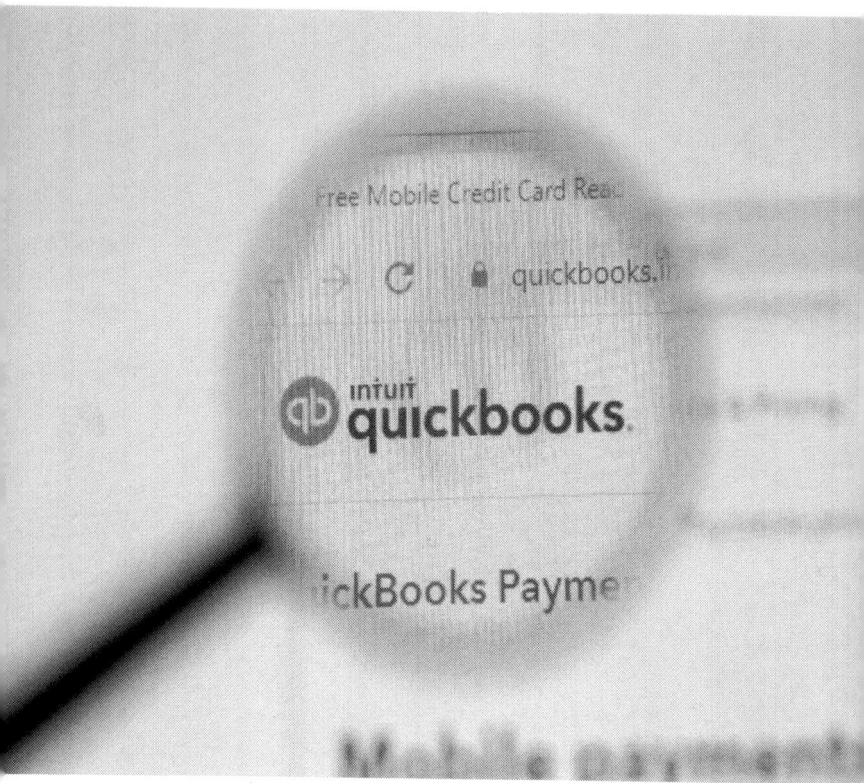

Have you ever thought about becoming an accountant? Not in the sense of a traditional CPA, but simply like a person who has to manage the resources to attain a goal, a business, a project, a life. Have you ever thought about this? It is common to enjoy achievements and to celebrate them, but all those not-so-enjoyable little bits of effort and discipline that got you to achieve something in the first place, well, those just aren't so popular, are they? They're the un-enjoyables. Yet, when it comes to bookkeeping and accounting, to ignore the un-enjoyables is the same as to condemn yourself to not knowing where you stand and where to keep going from there.

Luckily, in this day and age, technology has the power to enhance any human being into a bit of a self-taught accountant. This is where QuickBooks comes in. Of course, a formally trained accountant could probably put this software to great use, but that doesn't mean that anyone else couldn't find it useful or even crucial too. Think of it: How often does it happen that a person who knows little or nothing about crunching numbers can suddenly dispense with outside help because by pressing a few buttons, they've effectively crunched their numbers on their own? It'd be quite a neat thing to behold since we're talking about achievements and all...

But you're already holding this book in your hands, which means there is no reason to remind you of the virtues of the un-enjoyables or about why QuickBooks could be the right tool for your needs. Instead, let's focus on what you will get from your reading.

First, for the sake of impartiality, we're not going to assume ipso facto that QuickBooks is the best piece of accounting software out there. This is precisely why Chapter One is dedicated to giving an overview of some of the features that QuickBooks offers, both vis-à-vis the features offered by the competition, as well as in relation to the main concepts of accounting itself.

Chapter Two and Chapter Three aim at giving you a first taste of what QuickBooks is all about, what it can do, how it works, and what you need to be prepared for when you're using it for the first time. The main and more detailed part of the book goes from Chapter Four to Chapter Six, where you will get an in-depth explanation of all the different accounting operations that QuickBooks is designed for, as well as a step-by-step guide on how to use them.

Finally, Chapter Seven is about understanding some of the secrets and most outstanding concepts of accountancy in general, and Chapter Eight provides a list of advanced tips, some third-party integrations, and common mistakes to avoid. With all these tools, you will gradually get ready for your grand task, which is to enter the world of bookkeeping and accountancy by intelligently employing QuickBooks as your primary tool.

Now let's get started!

CHAPTER ONE

SHOULD YOU CHOOSE QUICKBOOKS?

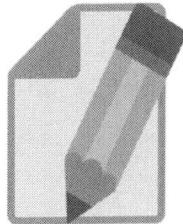

What is Bookkeeping

Any exchange in the financial arena represents information that one has to record in one way or another. This is the fundamental notion behind any bookkeeping-related activity. To record information and form the bulk of all gathered information, to build up a repository. Why? Because by knowing all that information, you can become a better decision-maker. It's like taking that ancient Greek aphorism, "know thyself," but taking it as a business philosophy.

Bookkeeping is also a preparation for the actual accounting process. This means that anything a bookkeeper does is a preliminary task. Basically, it involves taking documentation for each individual financial transaction that took place and recording it in a journal.

Every entry that the bookkeeper inputs can be recorded with one of two methods: the single-entry or the double-entry method. A good way of understanding what they're about is noticing that, in reality, anyone starts by intuitively using the single-entry method for things like personal finances, for instance. As its name indicates, this method requires you to make only one entry for every financial transaction. Either when spending or receiving money, the single-entry method is pretty straightforward in that regard because it records all transactions equally. However, its very simplicity can become its potential danger.

Single-entry bookkeeping is commonly seen as acceptable for small or individual businesses only. Any business that involves a high volume of transactions will be better off using the double-entry method, and even small ones would be wise to adopt it. The general opinion is that the single-entry method can lead to errors, and even to fraud, a lot more frequently than the double-entry method. Since it requires only one entry and, therefore, has no way of correlating with a corresponding account, it can be very easy for people to ignore whether their journal balances or not. In fact, the guidance for standard procedures, known as the Generally Accepted Accounting Principles (GAAP), mandates that all publicly traded companies must use the double-entry method.

As soon as you find a financial transaction organized into debits and credits, you can be sure that you are in front of a double-entry method of bookkeeping. In this method, every transaction is a double-entry transaction because it responds to changes in both directions. So the function of these two concepts, debits and credits, is merely to represent the two halves of a transaction, meaning that each one has a corresponding entry both on the debit and the credit categories.

Afterward, these records must get classified. From that point on, an accountant takes over to compile all the information the bookkeeper prepared and deliver it again in a variety of ways.

What is Accounting?

Whereas a bookkeeper is in charge of recording every financial transaction that a business has, the accountant is in charge of interpreting that information and compiling it in all sorts of different reports. Remember, the goal is to build a repository, a foundation of knowledge upon which to base any decision, be it small or big. The goal is to turn this into a constant practice, something you've gotten used to, and miss whenever it's gone.

For example, some of the reports that an accountant prepares can be delivered to investors who want to evaluate a business's performance before they decide whether to invest in it. If you have already grown a business up to a point and are in search of investors, it won't be difficult to see why this is important. Reports can be given to auditors who investigate for irregularities or to managers who will use them to determine future directions to take. So as you can see, avoiding problems and foreseeing new possibilities are much more reachable goals when you track your numbers constantly and in an organized manner.

Bookkeeping and accounting are often referred to as one and the same. In reality, they complement each other. The first one keeps the records, and the second analyzes them. It doesn't matter much if you find them explained under a single name. Once you have these concepts well understood, you will be able to identify them anywhere.

How are bookkeeping and accounting tied together? Apart from being two consecutive phases of the same job, there is a general principle that connects them theoretically, as it were, as parts of an equation that will be familiar to any accountant you ask.

The main principle throughout the bookkeeping and accounting processes is known as the Accounting Equation. This equation declares that in all cases, the following relation will be true:

Assets = Liabilities + Equity

Here is a brief definition of the concepts included in the equation.

- Assets refer to all the property that a business owns.

- Liabilities refer to all the debt that a business owes.

- Equity refers to ownership of assets tied to liabilities.

The accounting equation is a way to visualize how these three categories affect each other during the natural functioning of a business. Did you raise your own money to start a business? That means your assets were funded with your owner's equity. Did you get other people to invest? That means your assets were funded with other shareholders' equity. Did you get a loan instead? That means your assets were funded with a liability.

Come to think of it;it is a pretty logical thing. Whatever growth you manage to create comes from a source. If you interpret both the growth and the source as accounts that are interconnected, then all you need to do is add to one side and subtract from the other, or vice versa. Hence the name: double-entry bookkeeping.

For instance, if a business seeks to expand its operations, it will have to record it under liabilities or equity, depending on how it funds the expansion. As we saw, if it gets funds through a loan, this should be recorded under the liabilities account. If it gets funds through investors, this should be recorded under the shareholders' equity account. And at the same time, because both sources would represent an increase in the business's assets, this should also be correspondingly recorded under the assets account.

That is why the double-entry method of bookkeeping and the accounting equation are tied together. For every change on the side of a business's assets, there must always be a corresponding change on the side of the business's liabilities or equity. This way, any time the equation presents a problem, which is to say any time the amounts on both sides of the equation do not balance, you can be sure that an error has taken place and needs straightening up.

The accounts that are typically included in each category may vary from one business to another but are generally several or all of these.

- Assets: Cash and Cash Equivalents, Inventory, Accounts Receivable, Property, Equipment.

- Liabilities: Accounts Payable, Notes Payable.

- Equity: Shareholders' Equity, Owners' Equity, Dividends, Retained Earnings.

It is important to note that, thanks to their double and opposite functions, the debit and credit entries have different effects on each side of the equation. Even in the double-entry method, a lot of mistakes often occur because of this, so it's vital to remember the variable functions of each kind of entry.

- All debit entries will represent an increase when on the side of an asset account and a decrease when on the side of the liability or equity account.

- Conversely, all credit entries will decrease any asset account and increase any liability or equity account.

Accounting reports, such as a Balance Sheet, a Financial Statement, an Income Statement, a Statement of Retained Earnings, or a Cash Flow Statement, all invariably stem from the accounting equation. In turn, the equation stands in faithful obedience to the double-entry bookkeeping method. For example, a Balance Sheet is nothing more nor less than a standardized presentation of the equation, specifically reporting the state of all three categories as of the latest accounting period.

How Is It Related to QuickBooks?

As you can see, bookkeeping and accountancy respond to a very well-known and concrete need: To really know a business in-depth so you can manage it with precision. Satisfying this need means that bookkeeping and accountancy are subject to strictly standardized procedures and terminologies, all of which are neither simple nor quick to learn. And again, this is where QuickBooks comes in, along with many other software solutions, of course.

In 1978, Apple launched VisiCalc, the world's first spreadsheet, that allowed people to keep and monitor financial books on a computer for the first time. A couple of decades later, in 1998, Intuit launched QuickBooks, at first as a desktop software with a single purchase price and later as an online monthly subscription as well.

Unlike VisiCalc, QuickBooks held its popularity and kept updating over the years until it became what it is today, a GAAP compliant service aimed at helping individual entrepreneurs, small and mid-size businesses with all the challenging tasks of bookkeeping records and accounting reports.

The thing is, though, that because of their challenging nature, these chores can easily lead to bad habits. They are cumbersome for the novice, monotonous for accountants, and time-consuming for both. It could even be argued that most cases of people who never update from a single-entry journal are a manifestation of this issue. The problem is that a lot of the accounting software didn't really open up to a wider audience until a few years ago. This line of software used to be designed specifically with accountants in mind, but there was absolutely no effort put in to make it accessible to the rest.

QuickBooks and other competitors in this segment have helped change this situation. Some are more user-friendly than others, but overall, they represent a pivotal point in the history of accounting. What is more, with the ever-stronger trend of going exclusively cloud-based, QuickBooks now offers a comprehensive cloud version of their software, whereas other competitors have ditched the old desktop option altogether.

For many, it is sometimes difficult to adapt to this new model. For others, the advantages are far too many to pass on. In either case, the moment you start having expenses and revenues, it will always be reasonable to come up with a way of recording these expenses and revenues. Sure, you can always get along with a spreadsheet or two, but the longer you stay there, the bigger the amount of data that you'll have to transfer when you change your mind.

Remember that whether you know it or not, the moment you start doing things in an amateurish manner, you have established a method that will be harder to switch from with every day that goes by. This is why it is a very good investment to spend a good amount of time choosing the right accounting solution to manage a business, especially from the start.

On the other hand, it is not as good to spend too much time doing things that accounting software can automate for you. Automation means less chance for mistakes like accidentally recording a transaction twice, which are common in repetitive tasks, even for the experienced. It also means that you can spend the time you save on other business-related activities that require more creativity.

What QuickBooks essentially does is automate all those time-consuming tasks so that you can see things from a well-equipped interface, go through daily operations with less pain and more efficiency, improve your chances to attract funding, and forecast your business based on a robust foundation of knowledge.

Is QuickBooks for you?

QuickBooks has years of experience in the field of accountancy software and gets updates every year. Across a host of fintech publications on the topic, it is currently ranked among the best alternatives of accounting software for small businesses. A recent *PCMag* article projecting the best accounting software for 2021 ranked it as the top contender over various others, such as FreshBooks, Sage, Wave, or Xero, stating that QuickBooks is "easy to use, well designed, and built to serve a wide variety of users."

To find out if this is true, let's compare these alternatives to a few of their most salient qualities.

- Budget

QuickBooks is generally considered to be one of the more expensive alternatives out there. Due to its wide popularity, its prices get constantly updated, but on the online version, as of April 2021, the software offers five different plans depending on the size and line of business, and this is how they compare to similar plans from the rest.

	QuickBooks Online	FreshBooks	Sage	Wave	Xero
Self-Employed	$15/mo	$4,50/mo (Lite)	$10/mo (Accounting Start)	Free	$11/mo (Early)
Simple Start	$25/mo		$25/mo (Accounting)	Free	$32/mo (Growing)
Essentials	$40/mo			Free	
Plus	$70/mo	$7,50/mo (Plus)	$30/mo (Accounting Plus)	Free	$62/mo (Established)
Advanced	$150/mo	$15/mo (Premium)		Free	

Pricing is different in the case of QuickBooks Desktop, though. In this latter case, the amounts are much steeper but have the advantage of not being monthly payments, which can be a relief. The desktop version has three plans, Pro, Premier, and Enterprise. Pro costs $199/yr, Premier costs $299/yr, and Enterprise costs $1275/yr.

- Features

QuickBooks is also considered a complete accounting software. It includes all the tools that one looks for in accounting software, such as invoicing, credit card payments, payroll, a wide variety of reports, inventory and time tracking, the ability to sync bank accounts, a lot of third-party integrations, both cloud-based and desktop versions and a mobile app.

By comparison, the competition doesn't quite check all the same requirements. For example, Wave is particularly interesting because it's completely free, although it's also more targeted toward freelancers, and the variety of accounting reports that it offers doesn't match that of QuickBooks, so it will not be a suitable option for all small businesses. The most user-friendly of all alternatives, FreshBooks, misses some important features as well, like payroll and inventory tracking, which again points to the fact that its target audience is freelancers and smaller businesses rather than mid-size ones. Xero offers a pretty complete array of options, but it's not that far from QuickBooks in terms of price, it adds additional costs for extra features, and its user interface takes some time to get used to. Sage offers a pretty complete package and is within that same price range too, but doesn't excel on ease of use, either.

Summing things up, QuickBooks does have a reputation for being expensive and even for not having the best customer service, but this doesn't obscure its merits.

In addition to being an old player in the field, QuickBooks is frequently regarded as the best overall alternative. It is not as intuitive and accessible as FreshBooks or Wave, but it also covers many more areas than them. It is just as comprehensive as Xero or Sage, but it also offers a slightly easier user interface.

You can find and compare a much larger variety of software solutions, but the bottom line is that when it comes to managing a business, accounting software implementations are a huge advantage. They have truly become a must in a business's repertoire, and regardless of whether you find QuickBooks to be the most appropriate for your needs or not, the truth is you should always incorporate some accounting software in your business.

Size

With that being said, keep in mind that QuickBooks, or any of the above, are not tools designed for big businesses. For example, a large company like General Motors probably keeps many sets of books and employs an entire army of accountants, so its software solutions must be accordingly measured in size and capacity. The fundamental thing to keep in mind is that QuickBooks is not meant for businesses of every size but is still a pretty flexible tool. It will adapt to your needs as a starting entrepreneur, but it will also accompany your growth up to the point that is not limited. And this is important to note because it means that by choosing QuickBooks at the start, you won't need to migrate to another software for a long time.

So, if you are a freelancer or have a small or mid-size business, then QuickBooks can really help you out. Later on, if the business has been going well and you're starting to wonder if it'd be a good idea to shift to a larger platform, then pay attention to these signs:

- QuickBooks is known to have difficulty tracking more than one branch.

- Does your business have one branch or more?

- Even the biggest plan that QuickBooks currently offers, QuickBooks Enterprise, has a limit of up to 30 users.

- Does your accounting team require more than 30 people?

- High-volume traffic can clutter QuickBooks or even cause errors.

- How many transactions does your business record per day?

- Extracting data from QuickBooks to add a little more finesse to your estimates and projections can be somewhat cumbersome.

After getting the hang of it, are you satisfied with QuickBooks' features, or do you feel ready to go more in-depth with your accounting?

Advantage of QuickBooks

- Popularity

Across the globe, but especially in the US and Canada, around seven million people currently use QuickBooks. This number is surpassed by FreshBooks, which over 24 million people currently use, but it is still indicative of its trustworthiness. By signing up to QuickBooks, you are guaranteed to have a big user base to share and ask questions, as well as a feed of updates and improvements that will not die out because of discontinuation.

- Evaluating expertise

A good way to assess whether someone is familiar with QuickBooks is to ask them to operate it and see if they know any keyboard commands. However, the company that owns QuickBooks, Intuit, keeps a record of each bookkeeper registered on it. Information like their certifications and performance history is put together in a personal profile and made available to their clients. This way, it's easier to check a person's expertise on the program before hiring them.

- Customization

When choosing an accounting software, an important question is to check if it offers good customization capabilities, that they don't involve complicated programming abilities, and that they don't interfere with eventual software updates. QuickBooks checks all these requirements. It gives you the option to customize fields, checks, and invoices, estimates, receipts, and more. Its customization features are fairly intuitive and stay the same during updates, as long as they're done by an admin user.

- Security

Especially in case you were to opt for the cloud version, it is important to be aware of the risk of cybercrime. It isn't that you're genuinely opening the door to dangerous strangers every time you go online. Just that having your data stored and transferred there involves certain security measures to take.

Some of the things to look for are high-level encryption, multi-factor authentication, automatic data backups, the ability to give different levels of access to every user, and tracking their activity within the software. QuickBooks covers all of these security concerns.

Disadvantage of QuickBooks

- Price

QuickBooks is definitely not the cheapest alternative you can get. Moreover, their gradual shift toward the cloud implies that they charge you differently now. It would seem that you pay less when on the online version, but if you add it up over a year's time, suddenly, it won't seem that way anymore. Sadly, this is true for basically every accounting software available nowadays.

- Customer Service

A common complaint that you will find is that QuickBooks' customer service takes days to get your calls back. Since its target market is businesses on the smaller side, this poses a problem because that is precisely the segment that relies the most on good 24/7 customer service because it can't always afford to pay for additional expert advice.

- Different Versions

The desktop and online versions of QuickBooks are not compatible with each other. In addition, after all this time, it has been reported that the online version keeps being somewhat behind by comparison. For example, complaints about limited report building options, inventory tracking, and customizable charts are not uncommon among users.

- User Interface

The most commonly appraised alternative for its ease of use is actually FreshBooks, but this alternative is not suited, for instance, for any kind of inventory-based business. The truth is, all accounting software will require you to sit and practice or even read guide books because their complexity goes in hand with their tasks. With a little practice, you will find that QuickBooks is fairly intuitive for those who are just starting to learn and offers an extensive array of keyboard commands for the learned ones.

- Syncing

It is also commonly reported that QuickBooks' servers can get a little laggy when there are too many active users. Also, that credit card payments can take two or three days after billing to get executed. Since there is a chance that customer service will be unavailable at times, this is certainly something you will want to keep an eye on.

Main Takeaways

- The more you know your numbers, the better you will manage your business.

- Bookkeeping is the process of recording financial transactions in a journal.

- Accounting is the process of interpreting all information gathered by a bookkeeper and compiling it in reports.

- Bookkeeping and accounting are two halves of the same job, and together they make sure that the business accounting equation balances out.

- Bookkeeping and accounting can be tedious tasks, and accounting software can help you face them in a better way.

- Accounting software has been around for decades, but it didn't become user-friendly until more recent iterations, of which QuickBooks is widely considered to be the best current alternative.

- QuickBooks' target market is smaller businesses and freelancers.

- When looking for the right accounting software, take your time and think long-term. It is always an advantage to pick a good one and stick with it.

In the next chapter, you will…

- Learn the differences between QuickBooks Online and QuickBooks Desktop.

- See the offers of each specific plan.

- Get my personal tips and recommendations before choosing a subscription.

CHAPTER TWO

UNDERSTANDING QUICKBOOKS

Should You Choose QuickBooks Online or QuickBooks Desktop?

As you have probably noticed by now, QuickBooks is unique in that it offers both a cloud-based and a desktop application. Why are there two options? As it was pointed out in Chapter One, in the beginning, QuickBooks existed only as a desktop package. As time went by and cloud computing went from being an option to being a necessity, QuickBooks released a cloud version of their product. At first, it wasn't as comprehensive as the desktop version, but of course, this is no longer the case, at least not entirely. Above all, the main difference between both options today is the payment method that each entails.

Now, the trick here is to realize that the online version, like your typical Netflix or news outlet of choice, is a paywalled service that you pay for each month. By contrast, the desktop version is a little more old-fashioned. It requires yearly payments that look considerably higher but can actually be lower when added over time.

All of this is not to say that there aren't any key differences to keep in mind, and these will soon be assessed here one by one, but let's take a quick overview first.

The cloud version is called QuickBooks Online (often shortened as QBO), and the desktop version is called QuickBooks Desktop (often shortened as QBD). Contrary to what you might think, one cannot use both alternatively but rather has to opt between the two options. QBO is a completely separate version from QBD. It is often said among users that QBO is actually being much more marketed by its parent company, Intuit, than its original counterpart. The reason for this is simple: Intuit earns a lot more from monthly subscriptions than from yearly optional updates.

It is possible to start on QBD and later migrate to QBO, though. You can always import your data from the desktop to the cloud, and this process will be automatic, even though minor double-checking and report comparison will be necessary to make sure that it's been properly taken care of.

Other than this, most of each version's first advantages are pretty easy to guess. Online requires nothing more than a browser and a log-in, and Desktop requires you to run the program on a computer. Along with the mobile app, Online makes it possible for you to assess your business on the go, whereas Desktop offers faster computing. Online gets constant automatic updates, whereas with Desktop you can update manually once a year. Online is accessible for all users of an account, each from their own device, and Desktop offers just some of the same comfort as long as you run it on an office server instead of a personal computer.

However, once you sink your teeth a little deeper into these comparisons, it becomes a little harder to choose between QBD and QBO.

Specific Differences Between the Two

- Mandatory requirements

The first thing you want to check is if both options are GAAP compliant. Well, in reality, there is no such thing as a GAAP compliant software per se, but if you ever happen to hear the expression "GAAP compliant," odds are that they're referring to this:

- The double-entry bookkeeping method.

- And the option for both cash and accrual basis accounting (which you will learn more about in Chapter Seven, but basically has to do with whether you book transactions based on the date of a transaction or the date that cash actually came in).

And in this case, you're covered. Both QBD and QBO have true double-entry bookkeeping principles and accrual as well as cash basis accounting. You won't be missing either of them.

- User Interface

In this regard, the main differences between QBD and QBO stem from the fact that QBD is a lot older than QBO and, therefore, has been designed with another conception in mind. They're the same program, but their styles are different. This becomes apparent from the moment you stare at simple things, such as their invoice layouts or their respective home pages.

QBO is said to have a more user-friendly interface and a faster learning curve. This is in part because, with the exception of a recently added Advanced plan, QBO has fewer features than QBD. It was purposefully designed this way so that one would complement it at will with third-party integrations. The overall idea goes in hand with another era of software development, one where you're not supposed to run a fully equipped tool on a personal computer, but rather access a much simpler, portable tool wherever you are.

On the other side, QBD doesn't come close to the number of integrations that QBO has, but it is a better-equipped accounting tool in itself. There are certain capabilities, particularly when it comes to businesses of larger size, that only QBD can offer. Because of this, QBD also takes longer to master, especially if you get to their biggest plan, QBD Enterprise.

- Pricing

This is a controversial topic among users. There is no doubt that QuickBooks is expensive, but the fact that it offers two different versions makes the whole question even more blurry. Companies like QuickBooks prefer cloud-based because it gives them a steady stream of income from all the monthly subscriptions. At the same time, QBO is bound to prove more popular among younger users, whereas accountants often prefer the thoroughness of the old QBD version.

The only trouble is that freelancers and other smaller users can benefit from QBD's higher capacity but will mostly find a suitable plan for their rather limited needs on the more expensive QBO version. This makes them practically bound to opt for the latter, even if their budgets are tight. On top of this, QBD gets yearly updates, but one can normally hold for two or three years without feeling a pressing need to update, thereby making a single hefty payment every three or four years, and this can make QBD even cheaper still.

If QBO is not as complete as QBD, then why is it more expensive? There are probably server maintenance costs and whatnot. Things that should be taken into account when on QBO, but all of that notwithstanding, its price is certainly a drawback. As long as they're slightly different products, any choice between QBD and QBO will have to keep that in mind.

For now, this is how their plans compare:

QuickBooks Online (QBO)	QuickBooks Desktop (QBD)
Self-Employed – $15/mo ($180/yr)	Pro – $199/yr
Simple Start – $25/mo ($300/yr)	Premier – $299/yr
Essentials – $40/mo ($480/yr)	Enterprise Silver – $1275/yr
Plus – $70/mo ($840/yr)	Enterprise Gold – $1655/yr
Advanced – $150/mo ($1800/yr)	Enterprise Platinum – $2035/yr

- Customer Service

As I mentioned, in most people's opinion, QuickBooks doesn't exactly excel in customer service. Frequent reports indicate that they take way too long to answer phone calls and help troubled users. However, and this is probably not very nice or fair, once you get to the bigger plans QuickBooks actually offers a pretty good dedicated assistance service. It's called Priority Circle.

This feature used to be available only for QBD Enterprise, but with the advent of QBO Advanced, you can now access the same complete and professional service on both alternatives. And the truth is, if your business is big enough that you had to get one of these bigger plans, you're probably going to appreciate the expert advice too. It can save you a lot of trouble. It's just a pity that it's not available for every one of QuickBooks' customers.

- Security

According to the *Journal of Accountancy*, cybercrime is one of the most important things to consider when shopping for accounting software. In the wake of cloud computing, this has become twice as true. Moreover, this single factor could turn the whole table in favor of QBO. It might well be true that QBD is cheaper and offers a wider array of tools, but when it comes to cybersecurity, QBO is certainly the safest of the pair. Or is it?

Opting for QBD means that you run the program on your own computer. In this case, whatever risk you might be exposed to relies solely on how carefully you maintain that computer. If you have a good firewall, or better still, if you're running QuickBooks on your own private server, then your chances of surviving a cyberattack are not so bad.

But things like a domestic firewall or a personal server just can't compare with corporate-level security, simply because that stuff is well within their bailiwick. When you opt for QBO, you get access to various impressive features that will really help you feel more secure. For instance, they transfer your data only through banking level encryption, they have strong firewalls and multi-factor authentication, and they rid you of the need to back up your files because their servers are constantly and automatically backing them up for you.

There is only one other aspect that could veer this away from QBO and in favor of QBD. When you subscribe to QBD, you can restrict access to your company files on a user-by-user basis. You can choose who can see what at all levels, but you can't do this on QBO. So if you subscribed to QBO and, God forbid, there were to be an insider threat in your business, even if you're the admin user, you wouldn't be able to stop it from lurking through your files. Only QBD would give you this option. Of course, right now, all this sounds pretty neurotic, but you never know.

- Features

Both people who are in favor of QBO and QBD have preconceptions as to what the other alternative offers. In a way, this is a generational split. Younger users understand the benefits of cloud-based work, but older users cherish the original version, and in this case, they do it for good reason. For a long time, QBD offered a more comprehensive package than QBO in terms of features. And although Intuit has lately changed this a bit with the launch of the new QBO Advanced plan, QBD Enterprise remains unmatched.

Some people will say that difference isn't as worrisome as the possibility of discontinuation. They say: QBD might simply stop getting any updates someday, as a kind of final step to join the cloud frenzy completely. But this theory lacks plausibility for one reason, which is precisely the fact that QBD and QBO have different offers. For one of them to disappear, they'd first need to homogenize. As of now, they're two products and one at the same time.

Let's start with what QBD and QBO have in common, then. They both offer detailed charts that display basic needed information, such as bank reconciliations, the typical accounts payable and receivable, and other basic reports. They both have bank feeds, although this feature used to work better on QBD, at least until the arrival of QBO Advanced. They both get regular updates, but QBO gets them automatically and on a weekly basis, while QBD gets them only once every year (that is if you happen to choose to pay another fee that year).

From that point on, more differences begin to emerge. For instance, when you subscribe to QuickBooks, if you get a QBD plan, you can open as many company files as you wish with that single subscription. If you get a QBO plan, though, you're limited to just one company file for each subscription.

On the most expensive of all QBO plans, you have access to as many as 65 types of reports. On QBD Premier, you get up to 72, and on QBD Enterprise, up to 150 reports. In addition, QBD offers tailored versions for specific business areas. QBO only has one generic version but can be easily customized for every need. It also doesn't include any inventory tracking features but has more than 600 third-party integrations with which to fill out any operational whole you might need to fill.

Some features that only QBO offers are international invoicing, access to a unique built-in lending option, and a mobile app. Some features that only QBD offers are batch entries, sales orders, and the capacity to manage a much higher volume of transactions.

The launch of the new QBO Advanced plan was Intuit's attempt to address this difference in capabilities, but for certain things, there is definitely no comparison to QBD Enterprise. In fact, this is the main reason why some people upgrade from one to the other. Any QuickBooks plan, be it Online or Desktop, clutters with traffic higher than 400 to 500 thousand transactions per day. QBD Enterprise can handle millions of transactions with no problem at all. Then again, most of the people who upgrade don't use a lot of features because of this. They just do it for the traffic increase.

In the end, choosing between QBD and QBO comes down to what your priorities are. If you are a one-person business that needs mobility and ease of use over everything else, then you're probably going to prefer QBO. On the other hand, if you manage a growing business that requires more complex accounting to match, then maybe it's time for you to move up to a QBD Enterprise plan.

- My Recommendation

To sum up, QBO is a cloud-based service with a monthly subscription and a generic design that is highly customizable thanks to built-in features and third-party integrations. It is pretty secure and gets automatic backups but misses some user restriction abilities. On the other hand, QBD is run on a personal computer or server and has a yearly subscription. It isn't as easy to customize but offers tailored versions for specific lines of business. It is also vulnerable to cybersecurity breaches and needs to be manually backed up, but it can limit local users really well.

Perhaps on the most important side, both QBO and QBD are compliant with GAAP and have good customer service once you start to get into the more premium levels. Also, the most expensive of the two is QBO.

Overall, if your interest in learning how to operate this particular accounting software is inspired by a more general interest in accountancy—and I reckon it would be ideal if it were—then you should try to use QBD. Granted, it takes more time to know it in-depth, and it certainly doesn't benefit one bit from not being available as a cloud service too, but it's the only one that offers a truly comprehensive array of accounting operations.

If you ask a younger accountant, chances are that you will be advised to do the opposite and use QBO instead. And this would also be good advice. QBO is a good product and offers certain qualities that would be nice to have in QBD. It's just that by settling on the more friendly option, you're also renouncing the possibility to know all of what QuickBooks has to offer. Furthermore, by starting with QBD, you'll see that even operating QBO in the future will seem more natural as well.

Don't relegate yourself to be a passive user. Explore and repeat every operation until you get it correct. Ask yourself what each operation does and means in terms of accounting. The more you learn about accounting itself, the easier it will be for you to intuitively understand QBD or any other software that you happen to try later down the road.

Main Takeaways

- The reason there are two versions of QuickBooks is that the company is one of the first in the accounting software business. It started with a desktop version, and as times changed, it launched an online version too.

- QuickBooks Online is the most expensive option of the two.

- QuickBooks Desktop is the most comprehensive option of the two.

- QBO is short for QuickBooks Online; QBD is short for QuickBooks Desktop.

- QBD and QBO offer a lot of the same things but are also different enough to be considered two separate products.

- If you really want to get the most out of QuickBooks, it'd probably be best to go with QBD.

In the next chapter, you will…

- Learn to create your first company file.

- Enter your company information.

- Start to get around the QuickBooks Desktop interface and workflow.

CHAPTER THREE

GETTING STARTED IN QUICKBOOKS

In this chapter, you are going to learn the first steps you need to set up a QuickBooks account and start managing a business. Before you can do this, you need to be familiar with some terms that every user knows, such as the lists, centers, toolbar, icon bar, and home page. These aren't accounting tools quite yet, just some ways of navigating QuickBooks Desktop in a comfortable manner. They are effectively what constitutes the user interface.

All activities inside QuickBooks are organized in centers. It's a way of compiling them according to what they relate to. You can visualize how the centers are related from the arrows that connect them on the home page, which is by default the first thing displayed. Getting a view of the centers is a good way of grasping the implications that each business activity has from an accounting point of view.

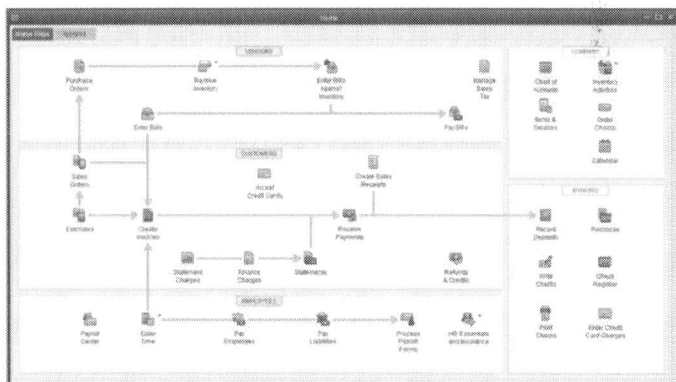

As you can see, the centers on the main display are these:

- Vendors Center

- Customers Center

- Employees Center

- Company Center

- Banking Center

Each icon that appears inside a center corresponds to a specific activity, and the arrows in between trace the path to be followed. A typical transaction would probably begin at the Customers Center, on the Estimates option. From there, it could go to Create Invoices, then to Receive Payments, and finally to the Banking Center, in the Record Deposits and Check Register options. A path like this includes every relevant process from the moment you give a service or product to a customer until the moment you put their payment in your bank account.

To make this and other transactions a standardized procedure that is easy to automate, another feature you will use are the lists. QuickBooks can store all kinds of data in lists so that you can access them from practical drop-down menus even in the middle, or rather, especially in the middle of other things.

Lists

Now, this is where it becomes important to think carefully about which QuickBooks plan you want to subscribe to. If you have QuickBooks Desktop, depending on whether you have a Pro, a Premier, or an Enterprise plan, there are differences to the limit of items you can enter in lists.

Element	Limit in Pro, Premier	Limin in Enterprise
Chart of Accounts	10,000	100,000
Names	14,500	100,000
Items	14,500	100,000
Job types	10,000	100,000
Vendor types	10,000	100,000
Customer types	10,000	100,000
Payment methods	10,000	10,000
Shipping methods	10,000	10,000
Payroll items	10,000	10,000
Memorized transactions	10,000	50,000
Memorized reports	10,000	29,000
Classes	10,000	100,000

You'll see that the limit in the smaller plans is pretty decent, but this is particularly important when it comes to businesses that rely heavily on inventory. Also, since QuickBooks is not designed for big businesses, expect the software to get a little laggy once you approach the thresholds.

The idea of this feature is to enter business-related information in the correct place and populate lists that are going to shorten your tasks when at work. You can do this either before everything else or in the middle of recording a transaction. You will find each list in its corresponding center, and easy-to-use drop-down menus will display everything you have put there, right when you need it in the middle of an invoice or some such task. For example, let's say you're going to purchase something from one of your vendors. You record the purchase and pull the items to purchase from a list, the specific vendor from another list, the account you want to pay with from a list, and so on. Instead of introducing this stuff manually every single time, you can choose from a list of everything that you've already used sometime in the past.

Toolbar

By default, every time you click on the Home icon, QuickBooks will bring you back to the center's display. This is the software's home page. As I said, there you will get a quick look at all the tasks that can take place inside each specific center, and you'll also have a row of buttons up above, which is the toolbar. If it doesn't appear at first, that means you need to enable it. Just go to Preferences, click on Toolbar and check the box that says Display Toolbar. It will look like this:

File Edit View Lists Favorites Accountant Company Customers Vendors Employees Banking Reports Window Help

Directly above the toolbar, you will see your company name on display, as well as the version of QuickBooks you've subscribed to and the exact location where you are inside the company file. One of the first things you'll notice in the toolbar is that the number of centers you have access to is now larger. There will be the same ones you could see from the home page, but also others, like the

Accountant, Company, and Reports centers. You can click on any of these tabs to access their specific options.

You have different options from the File button. For example, you can import web connect files directly from the software to ease the transaction process with your bank. You can create a new company file from there, just open an existing one, or even close the file you have currently open without shutting down QuickBooks as a whole. You can also generate a backup of your company file to save it on a different hard drive. You can restore a previous backup to maybe compare with the current one or even sync a company file to be able to send it to an accountant. If in QBD, there is the option to toggle between different QuickBooks editions. This, by the way, doesn't mean you'd be changing your type of subscription, simply that your subscription offers a variety of preset layouts to better serve your needs depending on your line of business. Of course, you can ignore this option if you prefer to configure QuickBooks yourself.

In the Edit button, the main thing is that you can access your file preferences. This is how you would toggle different displays on and off and basically choose and customize every area to your choosing. Another useful feature is you can click on the Find option from there, to locate the information you've forgotten where you put it. You would enter a specific number from a form, a last name, or something along those lines, and click on Find to see what QuickBooks has in store according to your search parameters.

In the View button, you can move the Icon Bar either to the left side or to the top of the screen. You can disable it to get a cleaner look and generally arrange the layout until it suits you. You can configure the Open Windows display in the same way. Its purpose is to let you switch with ease between all the different tasks that you might have used recently. This can simplify your user experience, but you can also disable it if you prefer.

Finally, the Lists and Favorites buttons. In the Lists button, as you might imagine, you can access all your lists. You can edit any item that is listed there, enter a new one, or delete it. This will also be available from all the different forms that you will have to fill out, but dedicated access just for it is available at the top if you need it. When you access any specific list, the display will show the current state of every specific item, for example, pending invoices, payments, etc.

The Favorites button is to give you quick access to those reports that you use most frequently and wish to put in a separate group. We will give a deeper look at this in the next chapter.

Icon Bar

Along with the Toolbar, the Icon Bar is another way QuickBooks has to get you quick access to the most commonly used features. It appears on the left side of the screen by default, but, as I said earlier, you can move it to the top or remove it altogether. These are all the tabs that it offers:

- Home

- My Company

- Income Tracker

- Bill Tracker

- Calendar

- Snapshots

- Customers

- Vendors

- Employees

- Docs

- Reports

- User Licenses

- Order Checks

- Invoice

As their names make clear, they lead to specific functions and tools. Let's say you want to go to the Reports Center, but you're currently filling out a Paycheck. Just go to the icon bar and click on Reports. Let's say you want to run a report, but you're not quite sure which one you need. Just go to the icon bar again and click on

Snapshots, which is a quick overview of business performance offered by QuickBooks. You get the idea. The same goes for every other option.

Okay, you now have an idea of what the QuickBooks user interface is about. Don't worry too much; you'll gradually get to know it better as you go along. The next thing is to set up your business information to actually start running your accounting tasks with QuickBooks. This will involve creating a company file, filling out the setup interview, getting an idea of every kind of form you can fill out, maybe populating your lists for the first time, and start working with this tool.

Creating a Company File

The first thing that will appear in front of you when you run QuickBooks is a window indicating that there is no company file open. Even once you have started to use QuickBooks regularly, you will encounter the same window every time. Depending on what you prefer and need, you can press any of the three buttons on this window:

- Create a New Company

- Open or Restore an Existing Company

- Open Sample File

Since this is probably going to be the first time, chances are that you won't have a file, and you will want to create a new one. However, it would be a good idea to open a sample file before creating your own. This way, you can try everything out and not worry about committing mistakes because you will start by operating fake data instead of your own. It's a great way to get a taste of QuickBooks before actually using it. You should try it.

After test-driving QuickBooks, the standard configuration to create a new company file has two initial steps. Let's start with the first step by pressing the Create a New Company button. This will take you into a second window where you will be prompted to introduce your company information, which is what QuickBooks calls their Easy Step Interview.

Easy Step Interview

With the intention of making the process of creating your first company file as easy as possible, QuickBooks has designed this first phase as an interview where you're supposed to answer the questions and therefore go on clarifying the type of business you run. Your sign-in information will be provided to you when you purchase the service, and then the boxes you will have to fill are these:

- Company Name

- Industry

- Business Tax

- EIN (Employer Identification Number)

- Legal Name

- Contact information: Phone, Business Address, City and Country, Zip code.

Some are pretty self-explanatory, but others might need a little explanation. Where it says Industry, put the line of business you're in. This will help QuickBooks customize your chart of accounts according to your needs. If you prefer to create your accounts personally, choose the Other/None option. If you're not really sure, click on the help button, and a window will give you a preview of the accounts that are included with each industry alternative.

When it comes to your Legal Name, you want to enter your name exactly as it figures in official records because this information will be used to populate various forms, so if you put a nickname or something like that, it can cause trouble. Maybe that goes without saying, but just in case.

In the Business Tax box, there are some options to choose from as well, again depending on the kind of business you run, which will determine the type of taxes you have to file. For small businesses, the Sole Proprietor and the General Partnership options will probably suit you best. Also along those lines, your EIN number, if you don't already have one, is a nine-digit number provided to you by the IRS, which will be useful later, for example, in Chapter Six, when you take care of tax-related withholdings through payroll. This box is for you to enter it once at first and not have to worry about it afterward.

Finally, you can fill the remaining boxes with your business's contact information. Once again, you can always fill it out later, while in the middle of an invoice, for example, but by filling it out here, you make sure that QuickBooks will use it to populate future forms automatically, and this will improve your workflow.

If any of these boxes were filled with incorrect information or you simply wish to edit something in them, follow these steps:

Account & Settings > Your Company

Finding Your Company File on the Computer

The QuickBooks interface will now display the home page in front of you. But before you go any further, it's good practice to make sure that you know where this new company file is stored in the computer. Otherwise, you'll know it exists, but you won't be able to open it next time. There are two ways in which you can do this. This is the first one:

File > Open Previous Company

When you hover over this last option, you should be able to see your recently created file there. Another way to find it is also in the File button. This time, click on the Close Company button and this will keep QuickBooks open but close your specific file. As I said, every time you log into QuickBooks, there will be a window saying that no company file is currently open, and right underneath that, there will be a list of the most recent files. Hover over yours, and this will show you the directory details of your file. Following them from the computer's native file browser means that you'll find the exact location where your file is stored.

Managing the Chart of Accounts

The Chart of Accounts will probably be pointed out to you as the single most important feature on QuickBooks, and to some extent, this is true. It's the reason why QuickBooks' initial interview tries to help you establish a set of accounts even before you've started to use QuickBooks. Every process that takes place and gets recorded in the software is related to some business account. Transactions are movements, and movements go from one account to another. Get this to run smoothly by starting with creating all necessary accounts and assigning them to the appropriate place.

You can access the Chart of Accounts from the home screen. To the right, in the Banking Center, you'll find the icon. The list that will appear includes all the accounts created for your business.

Over to the right, you'll see a column that says Type. This has to do with something you've already learned by now, in Chapter One, which is the accounting equation. This equation determines the type to which every account belongs, so you'll basically have asset accounts, liability accounts, and equity accounts. Of course, there can be lots of different sub-accounts, and the general idea is that some of them are for income and some are for expenses, but this is more or less how they will be arranged in general.

Creating Accounts

To create a new account, just right-click anywhere on the list, then click on New, or go to the bottom and click on the Account button to get the same option. This will bring up a new window asking you to indicate the type of the new account, whether it's for income or expenses, and whether it's a Fixed Asset, Bank, Loan, Credit Card, or Equity account. Click on Continue, and in the next window, you can give a name to the account, as well as a description, an account, and a routing number if you wish. At the bottom, click on the Enter Company Balance to put an opening balance for the account.

In the next window, you will be asked to indicate the statement ending balance and date. The first one of these refers to the net residue in a given account, and the second refers to a specific date on which an account's statement is issued, for instance, the beginning of the fiscal year. Check these two pieces of information and put them in their respective boxes, and then click OK. Go to the bottom again and alternately click on Save & Close if you're done, or click on Save & New if you want to create another account right away.

Now, given that accounts obey the accounting equation, after creating a new account, you'll find that another one figures there as well, being the counterpart. For example, if the account you created was a bank account, then it would be a credit account, and this would cause another debit account with the exact same balance.

Types of Accounts

The types in which your accounts get grouped become a little more complex once you go along. Let's have a quick look at some of the types that you may encounter or need while running your business.

Let's say you have certain equipment that is necessary for the business that you run, like furniture, vehicles, or machinery. These represent an asset, but not in the same way as the products that you sell because the former will stay in place, whereas the latter will keep flowing out of your inventory continuously. The name you must give to assets that are part of your work but not part of your trade is Fixed Assets, and you have to open a specific account for them. Since they are probably a variety of things, you can organize them in groups according to their kind and then ask for advice from an accountant on how to appraise them, account for depreciation, etc. This is generally something you'd better not do alone, at least not the first time.

Quite logically, then, all other assets that get sold and purchased that are not part of your operational equipment are to be called Other Assets or Liquid Assets. You can choose whichever name you prefer at the time you create the accounts. Both these types of assets are going to be grouped as accounts of the asset type. They will have a counterpart on the side of equity because that's how the equation works, but now you know that it is important not to mix them up but rather keep them in specific asset sub-accounts.

Similarly, you can create dedicated accounts for the cost of the goods you sold, which are called precisely that, Cost of Goods Sold (or COGS, for short). These refer to the costs incurred during the production of goods and products, like the labor and the raw materials that were needed for it. Any COGS account is an expense account because it subtracts from your gross earnings. The simplest way to realize how this works is to imagine a smaller example. Let's say you sell chairs at $50, and the wood and labor that goes into each chair represent $20. The gross profit from each sale will be $50, and this will be recorded in the income accounts, but to get the net profit, you need to calculate the gross profit minus the COGS. Therefore, what ultimately goes down as a profit will always be a little less than the retail price.

Liability accounts are to record amounts of money that you owe. If you have a credit card to pay for certain things, the payments you make with it are going to be a debt. If you get a loan to open a new store or expand your production, this will also be a debt. This type of expense will not be a regular expense but rather a liability. On the other hand, if you offer certain clients the option to pay you gradually, that means your business offers liabilities, too. So, whether it's for payments you owe or payments you are owed for, you want to create two separate liability accounts to take care of that.

Equity accounts can be used when an owner or shareholder retrieves or gives money related to a business. It might seem counterintuitive at first, but your business balance is not to get mixed with your personal balances, however small your business is. What you have to do is to create specific equity accounts to record transactions every time you take money away or put money in. In QuickBooks, these are called contributions and distributions. When an owner or shareholder takes money away, record it in the distributions equity account. And when they put money in, record it in the contributions equity account instead.

Other more regular accounts are, for example, the savings accounts. Those are going to be useful both for expenses and income. They are places for you to put cash collected from invoices and to get cash to pay for your own bills.

The QuickBooks Workflow

In the next two chapters, you're going to get familiarized in detail with all the stages of the process of recording and supervising business transactions in QuickBooks. However, suffice it to say right now that these centers we talked about at the beginning play a major role in the overall workflow. They are illustrated with icons and arrows that are intended to help you find the right direction with great ease, even from the first time. Get to know them well, and you'll always know where you are and what to do. The three main centers, Vendors, Customers, and Employers, where all of your transactions will take place, are to the left. And to the right are two more centers, one for the business itself, called the Company Center, and another for checks, deposits, and bank reconciliations, called the Banking Center.

Main Takeaways

- Your primary tools to explore the QuickBooks interface are the features called Centers, the Home Page where these centers are on display, the Lists, the Toolbar, and the Icon Bar.

- Creating a company file and filling out the initial interview are the first steps to running your business along with QuickBooks.

- Some of the answers you give in the initial interview can determine the presets that QuickBooks displays for you at first. If you prefer to change this later on, you can do so by going to the File button over in the toolbar.

In the next chapter, you will…

- Learn what are some of the reports that you can run on QuickBooks.

- What their specific uses and benefits are.

- How to find them from different places.

- How to set parameters in them, customize and memorize them for later use.

CHAPTER FOUR

MANAGEMENT

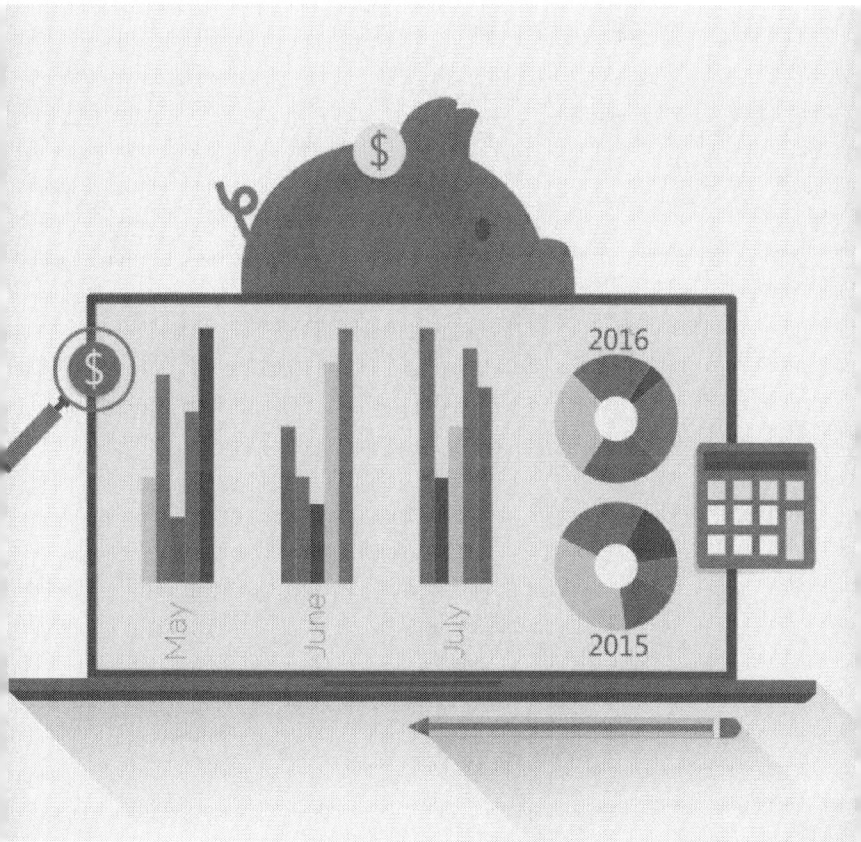

In this chapter, you are going to learn everything related to assessing your data in QuickBooks Desktop, from running some of the available reports and learning what they are for, to customizing them and looking at the standard options or those contributed by other users. On each individual explanation, there will be a quick arrow scheme illustrating what steps you need to follow in order to access and run the report in question. Like this:

Example > Of a Step By Step > Instruction

As I said, QBD is organized in centers. There is a center for each relevant phase of the production chain, so to speak, but some centers, like the Vendors, Customers, Employees, Company and Banking centers, can be found from the home page display or the toolbar, which is the row of buttons located on top. However, the Reports Center is different. It isn't displayed on the home page, but you have quick access to it in two ways as well, either by clicking Reports on the icon bar on the left or from the toolbar. Both paths lead to the same function.

Once in the Reports Center, you will find all available options arranged in a list of categories. When you access a certain report category, all the options included in it are displayed on the center. Below each report preview, you will find a short explanation of it and the option to choose a specific date range, mark it as a favorite, and run the report. In addition to this, you can also tweak your reports and save them as customized presets for later use.

Main Reports

These are the reports that accounting practice uses most frequently. They are the fastest way to get a grasp of how the bookkeeping and accounting jobs take place inside of QuickBooks. It's also necessary to run these reports on a quarterly as well as an annual basis because government authorities regularly request these. Finally, they are useful tools for you to evaluate a business's performance.

- Balance Sheet

Run this specific report by following these steps:

Reports > Company & Financial > Balance Sheet Standard

When you look at this report, the question you seek to answer is: How is my business doing right now? Or maybe: How was my business doing a couple of months ago? A Balance Sheet, therefore, is meant to illustrate the financial state of a business at a single given point in time. As said in Chapter One, the Balance Sheet is a formal way of presenting the accounting equation (Assets = Liabilities + Equity), and this is precisely why the areas that it has are the same, one for assets, one for liabilities, and another for owners' or shareholders' equity.

This is an example of how a Balance Sheet would look like on QBD:

Summary Balance Sheet
As of December 15, 2012

	Dec 15, 12
ASSETS	
Current Assets	
Checking/Savings	105,511.26
Accounts Receivable	19,627.31
Other Current Assets	67,035.85
Total Current Assets	192,174.42
Fixed Assets	90,201.88
TOTAL ASSETS	**282,376.30**
LIABILITIES & EQUITY	
Liabilities	
Current Liabilities	
Accounts Payable	4,059.17
Credit Cards	1,249.12
Other Current Liabilities	106,071.98
Total Current Liabilities	111,380.27
Total Liabilities	111,380.27
Equity	170,996.03
TOTAL LIABILITIES & EQUITY	**282,376.30**

As you may observe, the total under Assets and Liabilities plus Equity is the same amount. This is the unequivocal sign that the accounting equation is correct and your accounts are balanced. Every specific name that you find listed under these main accounts is, of course, going to be different depending on the accounts you created at the start. Also, the simple reason for having some elements labeled as Current and others as Other is that you want to distinguish between amounts that are expected to be covered in the next 12 months or later. You label as Current those that have to be paid in the next 12 months, and by default, you label all the rest as Other. You will find a more extensive explanation of this and other accounting concepts in Chapter Seven: Getting Started with Accounting.

- Profit & Loss

Reports > Company & Financial > Profit & Loss

This report can also be called an Income Statement. When looking at it, what you want to find out is whether your business is profitable or not. A Profit & Loss report, or Income Statement, summarizes your business's income and expenses over a specific period, then puts them one against the other and determines by contrast if the business was profitable during the specified timeframe.

It's similar to a Balance Sheet in that it shows your business performance, yet it doesn't do this for a single moment, but rather over time. This is why you will probably find that a Balance Sheet is informally thought of as a photograph of your business, because it gives you a kind of still image of it, whereas a Profit & Loss would be more like a video because its aim is to show progress over time.

This is an example of how a Profit & Loss report would look like on QBD:

Profit & Loss
December 1 - 15, 2013

	Dec 1 - 15, 13
Ordinary Income/Expense	
Income	
40100 · Construction Income	
40110 · Design Income	3,000.00
40130 · Labor Income	20,378.00
40140 · Materials Income	12,401.91
40150 · Subcontracted Labor Income	15,461.25
Total 40100 · Construction Income	51,241.16
40500 · Reimbursement Income	
40520 · Permit Reimbursement Income	0.00
Total 40500 · Reimbursement Income	0.00
Total Income	51,241.16
Cost of Goods Sold	
50100 · Cost of Goods Sold	3,610.50
54000 · Job Expenses	
54200 · Equipment Rental	1,550.00
54300 · Job Materials	9,045.86
54400 · Permits and Licenses	175.00
54500 · Subcontractors	5,837.00
54520 · Freight & Delivery	69.60
Total 54000 · Job Expenses	16,677.46
Total COGS	20,287.96
Gross Profit	30,953.20

At the bottom of this report, you will find a row indicating the business's gross profit. What this represents is the difference between its revenue and the expenses related to the goods that it sold. That is, total income minus the total cost of goods sold (COGS). If you take these two amounts from the example and subtract them, you will get the same amount that figures under gross profit.

A negative gross profit value would indicate that there is a problem because the business spends more than what it earns, either by inefficiency or other factors, some of them even outside of its control. However, you should keep in mind that QBD runs on the accrual accounting method by default, which means that it can record entries even when money hasn't been exchanged yet. For instance, you could be getting a negative value due to credit purchases that take more time to be reconciled. In such cases, just switch to the cash basis method, which you will find at the top of the window, right beside the option for the accrual method.

- Statement of Cash Flows

Reports > Company & Financial > Statement of Cash Flows

As you know by now, business is a chain of transactions that have to be recorded. Every transaction will either be an inflow or an outflow of cash and cash equivalents. These can be due to invoices you send to customers, purchase orders sent to providers, etc. The Statement of Cash Flows presents both inflows and outflows in a chart to satisfy two goals. The first one is to let you see how much liquidity is available to plan debt payments and productivity increases, and the second is to let investors see how solid a business is, to help them decide whether or not to invest.

Net income is not an accurate representation of net cash. Therein lies the difference between a Statement of Cash Flows and other reports. What does this mean?

Contrary to a Balance Sheet or a Profit & Loss report, a Statement of Cash Flows does not account for transactions related to credit. This again has to do with the accrual accounting method, which records transactions even if they take place in the future. For example, a rent payment might take place once every three months, but in your books gets recorded three times anyway, one for each month. Because of this, such an expense would not be properly shown in a Statement of Cash Flows. All you'd be able to see with it is that in the third month, a certain amount of cash went out to cover the rent.

Together, the Balance Sheet, the Profit & Loss report, and the Statement of Cash Flows are the three most important reports in accountancy. It is also mandatory to implement them in your business management.

- General Ledger

Reports > Accountant & Taxes > General Ledger

Remember that bookkeeping is the process of recording all financial transactions in a journal? Well, this journal is also known as the company's general ledger. Very few businesses keep their books on paper nowadays, but the main concept of a general ledger remains. And since it is the source of all the data that makes other reports possible, the general ledger is of the utmost importance.

In your case, the QuickBooks software as a whole is what you would consider your general ledger, but the exact point of attention would be the Company Center, specifically your Chart of Accounts. As it was pointed out, the Chart of Accounts is a list of all your accounts. It is where they are all recorded and stored, together with beginning and ending balances.

This is how a General Ledger report looks like on QBD:

General Ledger
As of December 31, 2016

Type	Date	Num	Name	Memo	Split	Amount	Balance
Chequing							102,820.85
Cheque	12/01/2016	136	Dobson's Properties		-SPLIT-	-1,522.50	101,298.35
Deposit	12/02/2016			Deposit	-SPLIT-	14,443.00	115,741.35
Cheque	12/15/2016	137	Sheldom's Software ...	2009 QuickB ...	-SPLIT-	-420.00	115,321.35
Sales Receipt	12/15/2016	57	Team Green.Bentle ...		-SPLIT-	2,159.66	117,481.01
Sales Receipt	12/15/2016	58	Team Green.Billing...		-SPLIT-	1,079.83	118,560.84
Sales Receipt	12/15/2016	59	Team Green.Canh...		-SPLIT-	2,159.66	120,720.50
Sales Receipt	12/15/2016	60	Team Green.Castle...		-SPLIT-	809.88	121,530.38
Sales Receipt	12/15/2016	61	Team Green.Carpe ...		-SPLIT-	1,079.83	122,610.21
Transfer	12/15/2016			Transfer Re...	Visa	-8,000.00	114,610.21
Cheque	12/15/2016		Team Green.Canh...		Accounts Receivable	-433.81	114,176.40
Total Chequing						11,355.55	114,176.40

You can find a General Ledger report by following the steps specified above, but with or without running it, you can access this information by accessing your Chart of Accounts.

Additional Reports

In addition to the main reports, you may benefit from other options. These reports can show you specific aspects that you may wonder about and point you in the right direction to locate and solve potential issues. For example:

- Accounts Receivable Aging Detail

Reports > Customers & Receivables > A/R Aging Detail

This report can answer the question: How punctual are my customers' payments? It is a way of organizing invoices according to the time they took to get paid, thereby letting you appreciate if your business suffers from recurring delayed payments or if it has a healthy flow of payments instead.

This is how an Accounts Receivable Aging Detail looks like on QBD:

A/R Aging Detail
As of December 15, 2017

Type	Date	Num	P. O. #	Name	Terms	Due Date	Class	Aging	Open Balance
Invoice	12/01/2017	118		Middlefield Elemen...	Net 30	12/01/2018	Landsca...		665.00
Invoice	12/05/2017	122		Paxton Consulting	Net 30	01/04/2019	Design		3,750.00
Invoice	12/10/2017	125		Loomis, Anne	1% 10 N...	01/09/2019	Landsca...		4,190.20
Invoice	12/12/2017	127		Hermann, Jennifer	Net 30	01/11/2019	Mainten...		35.00
Invoice	12/14/2017	130		Jim's Family Store	Net 30	01/13/2019	Landsca...		1,833.37
Invoice	12/01/2017	119		Theurer-Davis, Vic	8% 30 N	01/30/2019	Landsca...		907.25
Total Current									35,610.02
1 - 30									
Invoice	11/16/2017	145		ABC Corp		11/16/2017		29	70.00
Invoice	11/16/2017	146		XYZ CO		11/16/2017		29	140.00
Total 1 - 30									210.00
31 - 60									
Invoice	11/03/2017	144		ABC Corp		11/03/2017		42	185.00
Total 31 - 60									185.00
61 - 90									
Invoice	10/04/2017	143		XYZ CO		10/04/2017		72	385.00
Total 61 - 90									385.00
> 90									
Invoice	08/01/2017	142		ABC Corp		08/01/2017		136	550.00
Total > 90									550.00
TOTAL									37,060.02

As you may notice, on the left side of the report, there are bold numbers: 1–30, 31–60, and so on. These are called buckets, and their goal is to arrange your due invoices according to their age. For example, if an invoice is 29 days old, it will go under the range that can contain it, in this case, 1–30. This way, you can get a general idea by looking at how low each invoice appears in the overall report.

- Accounts Payable Aging Detail

Reports > Vendors & Payables > A/P Aging Detail

This report fulfills pretty much the same function as the previous one, except in this case, it does so for payments that your business has to make. In the same way, it organizes payments according to their age, so you can prioritize those that are most urgent and avoid delayed payments of your own.

This is how an Accounts Payable Aging Detail looks like on QBD:

A/P Aging Detail
As of December 20, 2017

	Type	Date	Num	Name	Due Date	Aging	Open Balance
Current							
▶	Bill	12/16/2017		Staples and Stuff	12/26/2017		200.00 ◀
	Bill	12/10/2017		Tennessee Tent Co	01/09/2018		340.00
	Bill	12/18/2017		Tennessee Tent Co	01/17/2018		340.00
Total Current							880.00
1 - 30							
	Bill	11/10/2017		Office Store	11/20/2017	30	35.77
Total 1 - 30							35.77
31 - 60							
	Bill	10/30/2017		Squeaky Clean Jan...	11/09/2017	41	250.00
	Bill	11/05/2017		Staples and Stuff	11/15/2017	35	100.00
Total 31 - 60							350.00
61 - 90							
	Bill	09/10/2017		Tennessee Tent Co	10/10/2017	71	110.00
Total 61 - 90							110.00
> 90							
	Bill	04/01/2017		Fishing Magazine	05/01/2017	233	50.00
Total > 90							50.00
TOTAL							1,425.77

Other useful reports are the different summaries that show you how much a particular client purchased or how much a particular item was sold for over time, as well as how much your business owes to specific providers and vendors. The steps to find any of these reports are detailed below.

- Sales by Customer Summary

Reports > Sales > Sales by Customer Summary

- Sales by Item Summary

Reports > Sales > Sales by Item Summary

- Expenses by Vendor Summary

Reports > Vendors & Payables > Expenses by Vendor Summary

Tax-Related Reports

QBD also has a variety of reports to help ease tax-related obligations. Keep in mind that you need to consult with official authorities concerning regulations relating to the location of additional and specific information, but these are some of the relevant reports you can use:

- Sales Tax Liability

Reports > Vendors & Payables > Sales Tax Liability

It has information on all taxable and non-taxable sales, sales tax payable, and collected tax. Its purpose is to show you a summary of all the sales taxes that your business owes.

- Sales Tax Revenue

Reports > Accountant & Taxes > Sales Tax Revenue

It is a complement to the previous report, a summary of all sales taxes that have already been paid.

- Sales Tax Summary

Reports > Accountant & Taxes > Sales Tax Summary

It summarizes the amount that was charged to each individual customer on the basis of tax, along with their personal information.

- Payroll Tax Liability

Reports > Payroll > Payroll Tax Liability

It has information on all tax-related deductions withheld during payroll. As a business owner or manager, you have an obligation to retain income taxes from each employee's payment. This report details all of these deductions, both those that are pending and those that have been made.

- Payroll Tax and Wage Summary

Reports > Payroll > Payroll Tax and Wage Summary

It compiles all employees' wages and tax withholdings at the level of State and local governments.

Favorites and Customizations

For quick access to any of the preset reports, without any extra customization of your own, you can save them as favorites. This is a way to filter those reports that you use most frequently and access them more easily in the future. In the preview of any report, you can tag any of them by clicking on the heart icon underneath. Doing this adds the report to your favorites list automatically, which you can find on the toolbar above.

Reports > Favorite Reports

Remove a report from this list by untagging it. Click on the heart icon again, and it will automatically be deleted from your list of favorite reports.

On the other hand, if you prefer to save a particular preset along with your personal customizations, the process is a little different. Right from the report preview, you can start by changing the date range. Once you run the report, you can access other options, like the ability to change the accounting method between cash and accrual basis, as well as the date range again.

If you want to access every customization option, go to the top left of the report window and click on the Customize Report tab. This will show a pop-up window that allows you to configure every detail through four tabs: one for the display, one for filters, another for headers and footers, and finally, one for fonts and numbers. After you set all of your preferred configurations, go to the top again and click on the Memorize tab. A new pop-up window will prompt you to give a name to your customized preset and save it in one of two places, either in a list of memorized reports or in one of the standard preset lists. If you choose to save it in the Memorized Reports list, you can find it later on the toolbar above.

Reports > Memorized Reports

Scheduled Reports

Naturally, it will eventually occur to you that since QuickBooks is supposed to help ease the accounting process, maybe you don't really need to run each report manually every time, and you won't be wrong. As long as you choose a pre-existing report, QBD gives you the ability to select and schedule anyone you want and to have it emailed to your desired recipients at the specified date. You can find this option on the toolbar.

Reports > Scheduled Reports > Schedule Setup

This will open a pop-up window with three steps. In the first step, you can check and uncheck the reports you wish to schedule. In the second one, you can give them a name and select the frequency, and in the last step, you can set the recipients and the details to be included in the email.

Comments and Contributions

You also have the option to comment on your business reports. Let's say you run a particular report, regardless of whether it was a standard preset or a customized one. When you have it on display, you can go to the top of the window and click on the Comment on Report tab. This way, you can hover with your mouse over any specific area of the report and click on it to add a comment for later reference. This option doesn't alter the report in any way; it just gives you the ability to save your observations on it and maybe share them with other colleagues. After finishing a comment, you can save the report and access it from the toolbar.

Reports > Commented Reports

QuickBooks' user base is another source of report templates. Take advantage of this, or contribute a template yourself, by clicking on the Contributed tab from the Reports Center. There you will find a regularly updated list of customized reports that other users memorized and offered to help the rest for free. Even if you weren't interested in using them right away, you could always find some are useful as a reference on how and why to customize your own reports. When you want to access a contributed report later, you can do so from the toolbar.

Reports > Contributed Reports

Insights and Snapshots

In addition to the options explained so far, QBD gives you a couple of ways to get a fast, more graphic, and more assisted overview of business performance. It is a branded set of charts that constitute QuickBooks' personal recommendation, what they consider you'd like to pay attention to. The first of these is called Insights, which you can find right beside the home page tab.

The Insights option displays some of the information you might be familiar with by now, but in a more visually attractive way. It starts with an illustration of your typical Profit & Loss report, but you can alternate between other options by clicking on the arrow buttons on each side. At the bottom of the screen, you will also find an overview of your recent income and expenses, illustrating them with colored percentages and even a pie-style chart.

You also have the possibility to customize your entire Insights layout by clicking on the gear icon on the top right, then checking or unchecking any of the options you wish to have on display.

- Profit & Loss

- Previous Year Income Comparison

- Top Customers by Sales

- Income and Expense Trend

The second set of charts is called Snapshots, which you can access from the toolbar.

Reports > Company Snapshot

The Snapshots option gives you a visual summary of your business's financial situation. It offers more or less the same as the Insights option, with the exception of some extra information, like an accounts balance, a breakdown of your expenses, and a list of delayed customer payments.

- Income and Expense Trend

- Previous Year Income Comparison

- Customers Who Owe Money

- Account Balances

- Top Customers by Sales

- Previous Year Expense Comparison

- Expense Breakdown

Ultimately, you might want to opt for QuickBooks' branded offers or go straight into the Reports Center, depending on how confident you feel at first. The Insights and Snapshots options are a bit less configurable, but they are a good introduction to what you're supposed to use QuickBooks for. Some of their features are the very reports that you will later run on your own, so it's always a good idea to start there and, as you get a grasp of the job, move on to running your own reports, memorizing and customizing them at will.

Main Takeaways

- The three major reports in QuickBooks and in all accountancy are the Balance Sheet, the Profit & Loss Statement, and the Statement of Cash Flows.

- Any report inside QuickBooks can be tagged as a favorite, customized at will, and scheduled to run automatically in the future.

- There are some predetermined options offered by QuickBooks, such as the Insights and the Snapshots, which offer a brief overview of various reports assembled all in one interactive and visually friendly display.

In the next chapter, you will...

- Learn the difference between estimates, invoices, sales receipts, and sales orders.

- Learn how to fill out a form for each of these different types of income transactions.

- Learn the difference between receiving payments and recording deposits.

CHAPTER FIVE

INCOME

In this chapter, you will learn everything that has to do with money coming into your business. The purpose of business is to generate profits, and this is possible either by selling a product or offering a service. In any case, this generates an inflow of cash that can be immediate or be divided into quotas that get covered over time. QuickBooks is useful in this sense because it lets you automate the process of recording all inward transactions, as well as track and analyze them in various ways. We just covered how to analyze them in Chapter Four, where some of the different reports that you can run are explained. In this chapter, the goal is to make you understand how to prepare things before any reports.

Estimates

For starters, let's go to the home page again, where you got this graphic representation of the regular workflow. In the Customers Center, to the right, you can see there is an icon that reads Estimates. If it doesn't appear at first, go to the preferences to enable this feature.

Preferences > Jobs & Estimates > Company Preferences

Once you do this, go back to the home page, and you'll now see the Estimates icon inside the Customers Center. This is where you want to start processing an income transaction. The Estimate looks a lot like an invoice, but it is the previous step. Let's say a customer calls your business and requests a product, but before purchasing it they want to know how much it would cost.

You would, therefore, provide an item by item detail of the requested product and its estimated total price, hence the name estimate, although it can be configured to whatever name you prefer.

After opening a blank estimate, you will have several different options. Let's go through these options one by one. At the top, you will find four tabs, Main, Formatting, Send/Ship, and Reports. The Main tab allows you to find previous estimates, create, save, delete, copy and memorize new ones, and print them or send them via email. It is also the tab where you have to introduce all information when you create a new estimate. The Formatting tab is where you customize your own templates, give them a spell check, add your business's information, your logo, and other information. The Send/Ship tab is to configure how the estimate is going to be sent or shipped to clients. Finally, the Reports tab gives you access to reports that are specifically about estimates for quicker use.

Back in the Main tab, to start filling an estimate, you will have three drop-down menus right below: one to choose the customer and the job, another to classify the job in a particular class of product or service, and finally, one to choose an estimate template. As I said, you can also customize the estimate same as any report, but the typical elements that it should include are these:

- Date (which is independent of the invoice date)

- Estimate number (attributed to every individual estimate so that you can keep track of them)

- Business contact and address information

- A detail of the purchased item(s)

- Quantity of each item purchased

- Cost, both individual and subtotal

- Unit of measurement (if you sell a product at a certain price per foot, gallon, or whatever measure you should need)

- Markup (overhead and profit margin)

- Sales tax

An estimate does not affect your account balances because it doesn't constitute a transaction yet. It is not even obligatory to have estimates before you make an invoice. It's a preview for potential clients. It can be stored before or after filling it out, and it can be printed or emailed to as many recipients as you want.

Invoices

The next step is to actually record a purchase. As you may imagine, you can do this straight from the estimate window by pressing the Create Invoice button at the top toolbar. If you prefer to bypass the estimate process, then you can go directly to the next icon in the Customers

Center, the Invoices icon. Let's go over these two options one by one.

If the customer approves an estimate you created a few days ago, you can click on the Invoices icon and open a new window. You will see that, aside from a few differences, it looks a lot like the estimates window. Both of them have a Main, Formatting, Send/Ship, and Reports tab. Both also have buttons to open a new blank sheet, to save, delete, copy, memorize and preview an estimate or invoice. One interesting difference, though, is that QuickBooks has integrated shipping tools, so you can log in to your FedEx, UPS, or USPS accounts without having to leave the program.

At the top left of the invoice window, you can pull the customer and job you want to invoice, which will open another window to choose from the list of available estimates. From there, you can decide to invoice the entire chosen estimate or just a percentage of it. Likewise, all estimates will appear on the list so long as there remains a portion of them to invoice. Another thing you can do is change the invoice from the basis of an estimate. You can add additional charges that will not alter the source estimate in any way, for example, shipping costs. You can introduce the quantity and the amount receivable for all additional charges manually or from the items list.

Some buttons are specifically important in the invoice window. With the Add Time/Cost and the Refund/Credit buttons, you can apply specific attributions to customers' purchases. For example, additional time-related costs, credits, or refunds that you might want to add to a particular job. With the Create a Batch button, you can send a single invoice to a whole batch of customers and split the total among them. This is useful, for instance, if there are multiple customers who are going to collectively make a single purchase. With the Progress button, you can track payment progress by checking which customers have already sent their payment and which haven't yet.

Once an estimate has been fully invoiced, it will no longer appear in the available estimates list. However, if there is no estimate you want to pull into a new invoice, then you can also create the invoice from scratch. This process is similar to the previous one. You will again have to pull a customer and a job from the drop-down list, same as with the items you wish to add to the invoice. After everything is filled out, click on the Save & Close button at the bottom right.

Sales Receipts

The difference between an invoice and a sales receipt is the amount you receive in payment for a purchase. If the customer is allowed a credit payment, you will create an invoice to charge them over a longer period. If the customer purchases something and pays for it at the same time, then you will bill them with a sales receipt instead.

In the case of the latter, inside the Customers Center, you will find the Create Sales Receipts icon. Click on it to open a sales receipt window this time, which again is going to be similar to those of the estimate and invoice. You can introduce the same things, the customer, the job, quantity, and cost. Just like in an invoice, at the top left, you will find buttons to indicate whether the payment you received was made through cash, regular or electronic check, debit or credit card, and even barter or a gift card. After all these steps, go to the bottom right and click on the Save & Close button. This will mean that you have actually recorded a sales receipt and received a payment.

Sales Orders

Before moving on to the part about receiving payments and confirming whether the corresponding deposits exist, let's have a look at some additional steps that you might have to use sometimes. Above the Estimates icon, before sending an estimate to the invoices, but still within the Customers Center, you will find an icon that reads Sales Orders. If this isn't the case, then it means you have to enable the option.

Preferences > Sales & Customers > Company Preferences

By the way, sales orders, which might seem a little dispensable at times, but can really help at least in a handful of situations, are a feature that is only available on QBD Enterprise. Other plans don't have it because it's a feature that is especially useful for inventory-type businesses.

Sales orders are necessary when you intend to sell a product in the future. For example, if a regular customer of yours makes various orders throughout the month, you may think it'd be easier to invoice them once but still keep a record of every order. In such cases, it isn't possible to invoice the customer. What you need instead is some kind of record that doesn't constitute a transaction but could eventually turn into one. That is what a sales order is for.

Customers can send you sales orders on their own as well. Since they aren't transaction records, you can make or receive as many sales orders as you want without causing any changes in your balance. And just as you would do with an estimate, it's possible to turn a sales order directly into an invoice or sales receipt. When doing this, you can choose which items from the sales order you want to transfer into the invoice.

You might be wondering why to use a sales order if all it is, is an unofficial record. Well, let's imagine that a customer wants to purchase a list of products from you, a couple of which you do not currently possess in your inventory. Naturally, you're not going to want to lose the purchase, and to avoid that, you will offer to order the missing products within a certain time. Of course, it will then be too soon to invoice the customer. Even if you gave them those products you do have, it would be more practical to keep another record of them and invoice the customer once the entire purchase is finished.

Also, with regards to this example, sales orders can help you get a better idea of the items that your business is currently missing and needs to acquire. It can help you budget according to the relationship between the demand and your stock, but without recording an actual transaction. In general, from the moment you start handling partial purchases, either to attract customers or to satisfy blanket orders, tracking your invoices and your inventory can become cumbersome. The purpose of sales orders is to help you face that challenge.

Receiving Payments

The last stage in the workflow of incoming transactions is probably everybody's favorite one: receiving money in exchange for your services. This part of the process is illustrated on the home page too. One of the steps is still in the Customers Center, and the other is in the Banking Center. If you follow the arrows, you will be able to see this clearly.

Back on the home page, then, underneath the Create Sales Receipts icon, you will find another icon that says Receive Payments. This is where you will actually receive and process all invoices and sales receipts. Click on that icon to open the Receive Payment window, which, not surprisingly, will appear fairly similar to other previous windows. But alternatively, before opening this window, you can set the account to where you want your payments sent. QuickBooks assigns one by default, called the Undeposited Funds account, and you might be better off leaving that alone until you have a reason to change it. In any case, here's how you can set your preferred destination account:

Preferences > Payments > Company Preferences

Back in the Receive Payment window, the first thing to fill in is the origin of the payment, that is to say, from whom you're receiving the money. Pick the customer and the job just as you did in the invoice window. This will display the total they owe at the top right of the window, and it will also pre-populate the payment receipt with all the currently open invoices that are recorded for that customer. By the way, don't forget that open invoices are those that still remain to be paid.

Right below, you can enter the exact amount of money that the client intends to pay. This will automatically check all of the invoices that this amount is sufficient to cover, and it will do it starting from the top by default. You want to keep that in mind because sometimes a customer might make a payment specifying that they wish to pay one particular invoice. What do you do then? Just uncheck all invoices manually and then make sure only to check those requested by the customer. After doing that, go to the Payment box and enter the amount that they wish to assign to each individual invoice, in case they also want to split the payment into more than one. It's important that you pay attention to your customer's instructions in this regard. If you don't, you and they could end up having to match different balances.

The next step is to enter the date and the payment method. Again, pretty much the same as filling out other typical records. The tabs at the top of the window are also going to be similar. One is Main, another one is Reports, and the last is Payments. The Payments tab becomes interesting, especially when you subscribe to Intuit's Credit Card Processing service, which is for customers to be able to pay directly from their credit cards. Bear in mind that enabling this carries an extra cost, though.

After filling out the whole receipt, go to the bottom right and click on the Save & Close button. And congratulations, you have successfully recorded a payment! If you go back to the Invoices icon and click on the one that was just paid, you will see that it now has a green sign that says it's been paid, along with the date on which the payment took place.

If you want to check this further to make sure everything's in order, you can run a Customer Balance Detail report, which you can access from the Invoice window and the Receive Payment window. Another way you have to check the payment is to go back to the home page and then over to your Chart of Accounts. Depending on what your initial configurations were, one of the two following options will be true. The first one is that you didn't change the default destination account, so your payment will get transferred into the Undeposited Funds account. The second one is when you did change the destination account. In this case, you would probably know by now because the Receive Payment window would have displayed a drop-down menu to let you choose what account you wanted to receive the payment.

The important thing to remember here is that whatever account you happen to use for payments, ideally, it should have a balance of zero. If you keep your books in order, you will make the deposits for each payment. Therefore your destination account will be regularly emptied because it's not meant to be more than a place of passage. So, after issuing your latest payment receipt, you can compare the amount that was transferred into your destination account with the one from the invoice that was just paid. Needless to say, the two amounts should match.

Recording Deposits

The next and final step after having received payment is to take it out of the intermediate account where it's been put and into the final destination account. This is because QuickBooks, as I said, has an Undeposited Funds account to record the payments you receive, but this account is not your bank account quite yet. The process of receiving a payment will not be fully complete until you take that money, put it in an actual bank account, and have a record of it in your checkbook.

Given that this is the last step in the chain of income transactions, it will take you away from the Customers Center and into the next one, the Banking Center. Avoid getting lost by following the arrows between the icons in the home page illustration that you've been traversing back and forth since the beginning. At the top right of the Banking Center, you will see the Record Deposits icon. Something you could run into when looking at it is the little red number floating in its top right corner. This is really intuitive. It has the same function it would have in any mobile app, except here, it doesn't mean that you have new messages. Instead, it shows that you have pending payments to deposit. It's important not to let that number grow. As you know by now, the balance in your Undeposited Funds account should regularly go back to zero.

Click on the icon to open the deposits window. What you will find in it is a list of all the payments that you have collected and haven't yet deposited, and if you wish, you can also filter them by the method of payment. The main idea, though, is to check the box next to each of the payments you want to add to your deposit. You can make a single deposit for each one, for all of them, or for a portion of them. It's up to you. Click OK, and the deposit chart will automatically populate with your desired payments. In each row, you'll see the information from each payment, the customer, the source account, the payment method, and the amount involved.

There is no obligation for you to deposit pre-existing payments only. You also have the option to make brand new deposits of your own, right from that window. Just click on a blank row and type your deposit information. Why would you want to do that? It could be that you want to record a particular deposit as an owner's contribution. Or you offered a rebate to a customer, and you want to alleviate this difference internally. Something of that sort would require you to make deposits without any previous payment.

At the top, you have the option to select the new destination account, and you're going to want to double-check that you picked the right one to avoid misplacements. At the bottom left, you will find a box that says "Cashback goes to." This is for what is called precisely a cashback, a small reward that banks customarily offer to credit and debit card owners as an incentive to use their product. However, in the context of a deposit, it could also represent a so-called distribution, like when the owner retrieves some money out of the business or maybe just a refill of your petty cash. These are just a couple of examples. In any case, it wouldn't be appropriate to record this amount as part of the deposit. By marking it as cashback, it will still transfer into the assigned account and be deducted from the deposit's total. The only difference is it will not be a new deposit on its own but simply a deviation of some of the deposited amount in a particular direction.

After filling out the deposit, same as before, click on the Save & Close button. It is also important that before moving on to other things, you reconcile your deposits with your bank account balance. Just compare both amounts and see if they match to be certain that no mistake took place during the deposit. And don't leave this for later. Do it right after making the deposit, or as soon as possible.

There are some common mistakes that could arise when making a deposit. It is important that you don't commit these mistakes, so here they are explained in bullet points so that you can revise them comfortably at any time.

- First Mistake: Using Check Register instead of Record Deposits

  You must not go to the Check Register icon to record a deposit directly there. If you do that, instead of going into the Record Deposits icon, as you should, the money you received from customers' payments won't be transferred anywhere. It will stay in the Undeposited Funds account and accumulate endlessly.

- Second Mistake: Recording a deposit twice by choosing an account from Check Register

  From the moment you created the invoice, QuickBooks already knows that a deposit represents an income transaction. Going into the Check Register icon to record your deposit means that you'll end up picking an account, probably an income account, and recording this transaction twice.

The bottom line is this: Stay away from the Check Register icon when in the last step of an income transaction. If you want to record a deposit, follow the arrows and do it from the Record Deposits icon. On the other hand, after making the deposit, you should move on to the Check Register icon to see if your deposit appears and has been recorded in the correct account.

Main Takeaways

- A normal transaction starts with an estimate, then becomes an invoice or a sales receipt, then the payment to cover for them is received, and a corresponding deposit is finally recorded.

- When the requested product is not in stock, you can record a previous form called a sales order, which is not legally binding but can eventually give pace to an estimate and start a transaction process.

- You should use invoices to record sales that are paid for later.

- You should use sales receipts to record sales that are paid for immediately.

In the next chapter, you will…

- Learn the difference between bills and sales receipts.

- Learn to place purchase orders.

- Learn all the details on how to manage payroll.

CHAPTER SIX

EXPENSES

This is the other side of the coin if your business was a coin. Remember, all transactions have one of two directions: inflow and outflow, income and expenses. The latter is obviously not going to seem as enjoyable as the former, but it is just as important. It can be more or less complex depending on the size of your business, but whatever that size is, you'll be better off knowing how to handle these chores cleverly. Trust me.

The type of transactions you will learn about involves everything from purchases that you make from your vendors to paychecks for your employees and additional expenses related to their withholdings. All this has a lot of specific details you need to be familiar with, so let's set every major topic apart and go through all of them one by one.

Entering and Paying Bills

Bills are, in a way, the equivalent of invoices, with some key differences. For example, the person who typically issues them. Both invoices and bills contain the same kind of information, the details of a purchase, the cost, the quantity, the sales tax, etc. Invoices are commonly issued by businesses to collect payments from their customers, whereas bills are issued to keep track of their own debts to vendors. To put it another way, if you provide a service and wish to get paid for it, you issue an invoice. If you make a purchase and wish to pay for it, you issue a bill.

Both documents also carry legal obligations. They are official documents that cannot be just canceled at will. That is why sales orders and purchase orders come in handy, as a kind of unofficial previous step. You have seen some of this in the previous chapters, during the point about sales orders. And finally, like invoices, bills are also more commonly used for sales that are provided with credit, whereas checks would be the preferred method of payment for things that are paid at the moment of purchase.

Make a bill in QuickBooks Desktop by going to the home page and over to the Vendors Center. There you will find that one of the first icons on the left is the Enter Bills icon. Click on it to open the bills window. At the top of this window, you will find two options to pick: bill or credit. Below this, you can enter the vendor manually or pull one from the drop-down list. When you do that, part of the bill will automatically pre-populate for you, for example, the area where it says the vendor's address and the payment terms, if these were already determined during setup.

The payment terms have to do with the amount of time agreed upon between the date of the bill and the actual due date. As I said, bills are commonly used for sales provided with credit, so they're payments that are programmed to happen over a set period. The exact time is probably around 15 to 30 days, depending on what you and your vendor prefer. So the idea is that the bill date is always the date on which you recorded the bill, and the due date could set itself through the payment terms or could be manually adjusted to a certain number of days after the bill date.

At the top, you have two tabs for different things to fill the bill with, one for expenses and the other for items. This is a way to organize your expenses according to what they represent to your business. For instance, if you want to pay some operational expenses, the kind that you get on a regular basis to keep everything running, like the electricity bill, then you can enter this in the Expenses tab. If you're paying for something less permanent, like a product that you're missing in your inventory, then you can enter this in the Items tab.

To the right of the bill window, you can introduce relevant data in case you're tracking job costing as well. All you have to do for this is enter the customer and the job that corresponds to the specific bill you happen to be filling out at the time.

Finally, you can check the box for every item or expense that you wish to mark as billable and add a reference number and a memo beside each one listed in the bill. The reference number performs the same function here as in any of the other documents that you have learned about so far. It helps keep track more easily and enumerates how many of each you have issued, although it is not obligatory to always fill it out. The memo is for you to enter any additional notes that you may wish to attach to the bill.

If you want to check that it's all been processed correctly up until this point, just run the Unpaid Bills Detail report, either from the Reports Center or from the bill window itself.

Reports > Vendors & Payables > Unpaid Bills Detail

Having done all this, you can go to the bottom right, click on the Save & Close button, and that's all. You have entered a bill correctly. Now let's see how to go about paying that bill.

Follow the arrows on the home page again, still inside the Vendors Center, and you'll find the Pay Bills icon. Click on it, and a list of all unpaid bills will be displayed before you. Go through that list and check all the bills you wish to pay. There are going to be several options to filter them as well, according to the date, the vendor, the amount, and many other parameters. To the right of each listed bill, you can manually enter the amount of money you want to pay, in case you want to pay just part of a bill. QuickBooks will keep a record of the rest.

At the bottom of the bills window, you have other options. The Go To Bill button leads straight into the specific bill you have selected to check its details or maybe edit them. The Set Discount button gives you the ability to introduce a percentage of discount to net 30, or any other term that suits you best. There you'll also have to introduce the exact account to be able to track the discount. The Set Credits button works if you've previously applied a credit memo to a bill. Let's say you did and want to select one in particular. Just click on that button to see a list of all existing credit memos and check the ones you wish to attach to the bill payment. Finally, click the To Be Printed or the Sign Check Number buttons alternatively, depending on whether you want to have them printed or just electronically stored.

After all these steps, as always, go to the bottom right and this time, click on the Pay Selected Bills button. Click OK, and that means that the bills you selected have been paid correctly. If you want to pay another group of bills right away, you can do that from the confirmation window, or you can go directly to check your newly paid bill. Do the latter by running an Unpaid Bills Detail report again. Another way is to go to the Check Register icon in the Banking Center and see if the latest paid bills appear at the bottom of that list.

You'll want to pay attention to what this last record says on the right. If it says "Bill Payment," then the payment was processed correctly. If instead, it says "Check," that means you might have recorded a bill payment correctly, but you created a new bill payment and didn't link it to any pre-existing bill. Remember, you want to pick an existing bill to pay for it, not create a new one and leave the previous one unpaid. Avoid this error by following the workflow that is suggested by the arrows on the home page.

Checks

Another way to make payments is to write checks. Of course, when you pay a bill, you're technically making a check too. So what is the difference between a check and a bill? The quick explanation has to do with the immediacy of the payment, or better still, with the part of a payment in which a bill and a check come into play. The bill is a document that indicates what you purchased and will have to pay for. On the other hand, a check is a way of paying a bill. That is why paid bills also end up in the Check Register. The main difference, therefore, is that a bill gets paid over time, and a check is usually identified with services that are immediately paid for.

Write a check in QBD by going to the Banking Center and clicking on the Write Checks icon. This will display a similar window to those for invoices, bills, etc. On the upper half, there is an interactive preview of the form you're about to fill, and on the lower half, there is a series of rows to populate with information to add to the check.

Click in the drop-down menu next to Bank Account to pick the source account from which you want to pull the funds to pay for the check. On the right, the box that reads Ending Balance will show you the latest balance of the account. Below that, there will be a box that reads Pay To The Order Of. That is where you have to enter the payment's recipient. When you fill that box, a smaller window will appear to show you all pending bills recorded under that name. Pick the ones you want to pay and click OK, then other boxes in the form will pre-populate with the recipient's information.

Normally, though, the check will be for a brand new payment that you'll probably make right then and there. In that case, enter the name of the recipient but do not choose any job or pre-existing bill. Enter the items you wish to include, their quantity, cost, and amount details, and you're pretty much done. Go back up to enter the date, the total amount, and the check number. After all these steps, as always, go to the bottom right and click on the Save & Close button.

Since both bills and checks constitute payments that are going to end up in your check register one way or another, you can go make sure that your check was properly recorded by going back to the home page, clicking on the Check Register icon, and looking at the last item in the list, which should be your recently recorded check.

Purchase Orders

One could say that bills are to invoices the same that purchase orders are to sales orders. What does this mean? Just that income and expense transactions are similar to one another, which is to be expected, and so most income transactions have a counterpart on the expense side. If a sales order is a previous unofficial record for a sale you intend to make, then a purchase order is the same, except in this case, it is for a purchase you want to make.

When talking about these kinds of unofficial documents, you'll be interested to know that they are commonly called non-posting documents, meaning that they aren't legally binding in any way, but just additional forms to help keep track of everything. This can become particularly useful for businesses that work on an inventory basis, with lots of physical products that they need to be tracking and keep in stock. These kinds of inventory features are a privilege of the QBD Enterprise plan, as I said in the point about sales orders, so if you really need it, then you're going to have to upgrade.

Once again, if you can't find this option, go to your preferences and enable it.

Preferences > Sales & Customers > Company Preferences

Go to the left of the Vendors Center on the home page and click on the Purchase Orders icon. This will open the purchase order window, which you can fill out as follows. Pick the vendor you want to buy from, the class of the purchase, and specify the shipping address if it isn't the same as your office address. After this, the vendor information box will populate automatically. You can add the purchase order date, and under the PO Number, put the purchase order number according to how many you've done so far. Again, keep in mind that this number doesn't need to relate to invoicing numbers or anything like that.

In the actual body of the order, pick the items you plan to buy from the items list and specify the quantity and the date. Besides that, if you happen to be placing an order for a specific customer request, you can link the order to it by adding the customer and the job in question. This will let you know that when the order arrives, you have to derive at least a part of it directly into that invoice.

After filling everything out, go to the bottom right and click on the Save & Close button. You won't be able to corroborate any change caused by the purchase order because, once again, it isn't an actual bill. It will not change the items list until the moment your order arrives. By then, the purchase order will turn into a proper bill, and only then will you detect a tangible consequence from it.

Credits and Refunds

There are other important functions besides inventory tracking and supply, for example, being able to offer customers all the typical ease that goes along with purchase information, like credits and refunds. You're not obligated to offer these comforts, but they could play a decisive role for your business, so it wouldn't be a bad idea to keep them in mind. Luckily QuickBooks can incorporate them seamlessly into the rest of the transaction process, and that is what this point is about.

In a nutshell, creating a credit or refund note is short and simple.

Customers > Create Credit Notes/Refunds

Or alternatively, you can go to the Refunds & Credits icon in the Customers Center and click on it. Both paths will lead to a blank window for you to fill out. You can apply the note to invoices and also to your own purchases from vendors. This will depend on what your agreements are with either of them. Enter the customer and the job to which you want to apply a credit or refund, choose the specific items from the items list, then go to the bottom right and click on Save & Close. That's all. However, keep in mind that credit essentially means an extension over time, and refund means giving back, again later in time, so you might imagine the tricky part comes when you think about what this credit or refund will be applied to. How are you going to keep track of it? It can take different directions depending on what you do.

When you click Save & Close, you will get a pop-up window asking you to choose between these three options:

- Retain as an Available Credit

- Give a Refund

- Apply to an Invoice

Each option will have a checkbox to indicate which you want to pick. The first option, Retain as an Available Credit, means that any credit you apply will be retained to be transferred later by the customer to whatever invoice they prefer. Once the credit gets applied to a specific invoice, you'll be able to track it for your balance. The second option, Give a Refund, is obviously not for credit, but it works in the same way. In this case, a new pop-up window will appear to pick between all currently open invoices for the customer you selected. Check those you wish and click OK. The refund will be attributed specifically to the invoice you selected. Finally, the third option, Apply to an Invoice, has the same steps as the previous option, only this time it actually is for credit to be applied to a specific invoice.

As you may be noticing, the gist of it is that you want to apply credits or refunds to specific customers or specific transactions, or both. Since these processes involve yet more information that will get extended over time, then it becomes important to avoid losing them by not linking them correctly to an invoice or bill. What QuickBooks offers is the guarantee that as long as you keep recording these notes and applying them to the desired customers, vendors and transactions, then the program will take care of remembering it so that you have no problem while tracking credits and refunds later on.

What Is Payroll and How to Set it Up on QuickBooks?

The last and probably most complex part of a business' expense transactions is payroll. Naturally, this is not going to be a concern for you if, for instance, you're a freelancer, but the bigger your business gets, the bigger the odds that you will have employees under your responsibility. This one factor carries a big change in the whole dynamic because it means you need to take care of their income taxes, medical insurance, social security, and other things that are easy to get lost in.

First things first. Payroll is the list of employees that your business is going to have and the amount of money that you have agreed to compensate them with after a certain period. This involves regularly setting aside a considerable amount of money to cover the total compensation sum, as well as tracking time for hours of work and putting away a percentage into mandatory withholdings for health, pensions, and taxes.

It is customary for businesses of bigger sizes to hire outside services that specialize in taking care of this, but when you're a small business, chances are you will prefer to reduce costs and take care of payroll internally. This doesn't have to be a bad thing. Good accounting software, like QuickBooks, is designed to incorporate payroll as one of its features so that you don't need to outsource it. If you have a QBD Enterprise subscription or if you get the specific QuickBooks Payroll service, then rest assured that your accounting solution has all the necessary tools to help you through.

These are the additional prices to keep in mind when getting the QuickBooks Payroll service:

Enhanced Payroll	$30/mo
Assisted Payroll	$54,50/mo
Assisted + QBD Enterprise Diamond	$211,50/mo

And before setting up the payroll function, you will also need to gather certain information:

- Get every employee to fill out a W-4 form, also known as an Employee's Withholding Certificate.

- Get every employee to fill out an internal form with all their personal information: legal name, address, the date on which they were hired, and their birth date.

- Get details of the specific deductions for each of your employees. These generally include medical care, social security, and income taxes.

- Get their deposit information, so you know where to transfer each employee's payment.

- Get every employee's ID and FEIN (Federal Employer Identification Number) to pay taxes.

- Establish a pay rate for each employee and also a payment schedule, so you know when their payment is due.

After doing all this, you can start setting up payroll in your business, which is a process that you can divide into these steps.

Setting Up Payroll Items

As with other options, get to the payroll option from the home page. Go down to the Employees Center and click on the Turn On Payroll icon. To enter a new item or edit a previous one, follow the steps and choose either of the two options:

Employees > Manage Payroll Items > New Payroll Item List

Employees > Manage Payroll Items > Write/Edit Payroll Item List

This will bring up the payroll items list, where you can find all preset items and others you created. Right click anywhere on the screen and choose the New option, then choose between the easy and the custom setup, preferably the latter. A new window will appear and take you through various steps. First, choose the kind of the item (wage, tax, addition, or deduction), then type the name of the new item, then enter the agency to which the payment will go, then choose the bank account to cover for it, then choose or create the liability account and sub-account where you want withholdings to go, set a payroll schedule if you wish, click OK, and you're done. The newly created item will now appear in the list.

Setting Up Employees

Go back to the Employees Center. You will find a list of all your employees, with an X sign next to those marked as inactive. When you click on a particular employee, you'll see below a list of all recorded transactions under the employee's name.

Go to the top of the window and click on the New Employee tab. A window will appear, prompting you to enter the employee's information, which you have listed above. The most important tab is the one that says Payroll Information. There, you can set a payroll schedule for the employee, the details of their earnings (overtime, vacations, etc.), payroll items that are specific to each employee, the bank accounts that will issue and receive the paycheck, specific tax withholdings, and compensations. After filling the form, click OK, and your new employee will now appear in the employees' list along with the rest.

Paying Employees

Go back to the Employees Center and this time, click on the Pay Employees icon. This will bring up the paychecks window, which can remind you of any scheduled payroll that might be due. In such a case, just click on the Start Scheduled Payroll button. Alternatively, you can click on the Start New Unscheduled Payroll button, and this will bring up another window. Choose the period end date, the check date, the source bank to cover the payment, check which employees you wish to pay, add any specific information to each one (overtime, sick days, etc.), make sure all added or deducted amounts are correct.

After these steps, go to the bottom right and click Continue. You'll see a detail of all net and gross individual paychecks. Double-check that everything is correct, and then click the Create Paychecks button. A window will pop up to notify you that there are new paychecks for you to print and sign. Also, you can go to the Check Register icon and see that each paycheck now appears at the bottom of the list.

Paying Taxes

All deductions are now going to be a liability for you. At the moment of making the paychecks, the specified withholdings will have gotten derived into a liability account from your business' chart of accounts. All payroll responsibilities will not be yet finished until you send them to their corresponding agencies.

Still in the Pay Employees icon, go to the top left and click on the Pay Liabilities tab. A new window will show you all current unpaid liabilities, together with amounts, due dates, and origin of the funds. Check the ones you're going to pay and click on View/Pay at the bottom right. Another window will appear to show you a preview of the check. You can fill and edit everything you see fit, then finally click on Save & Close. This will appear on your Check Register as well, and that means that all payroll-related expenses are taken care of.

Main Takeaways

- The difference between bills and checks is similar to that of invoices and sales receipts, but for expense transactions. That is to say, you should use bills to record purchases that you pay for later and use checks for purchases you pay immediately.

- Purchase orders are issued to request products from vendors, generally to refill inventory stock, and same as sales orders, they are not yet legally binding.

- Credits and refunds are to be attributed to specific customers, items, or transactions. By enabling those functions, QuickBooks helps you keep track of them from beginning to end.

- Payroll is probably the most complex type of expense transaction you can face. Setting it up carefully on QuickBooks will help automate most of it and avoid mistakes.

In the next chapter, you will…

- Go back through some accounting principles, having now given the first steps towards using QuickBooks.

- Learn some additional concepts that will provide perspective to what you can do with QuickBooks.

- Learn how to interpret reports.

CHAPTER SEVEN

GETTING STARTED WITH ACCOUNTING

This chapter is to look back at some of what has been said up to here, but from the point of view of accounting with or without QuickBooks. Accounting is this arcane process that was invented thousands of years ago and acquired its most modern appearance some five centuries ago, among the bankers and merchants of Italy. It is widely agreed that the double-entry method of bookkeeping, which you're already acquainted with, started to get its widespread standard status during that period. From that moment on, accounting became more and more a language of its own. It involved a lot of terms and concepts that were part of a specialized job, one that no one else could understand easily. However, the methods and concepts have thrived until the modern age because business management, if anything, is even more popular nowadays.

As currently understood, accounting is a process that accompanies business activities in the pursuit of organizing, interpreting, and forecasting transaction behavior. It involves recording transactions, checking account balances, analyzing the recorded information, and using it to assemble reports to deliver to owners, managers, or investors. Accounting is a part of the decision-making process, then. Investors contribute with cash funds, businesses operate to produce revenue, and accounting provides the knowledge of everything that takes place.

So what is the relationship between business management and accounting? It comes down to time and cash. Whenever you're starting a business, whenever you've had a business for years or at any point in between, all there is at your disposal is time. If you're lucky, cash will be available too, but more often than not, it won't be, so you have to decide how to use whatever limited cash you have through time. That is, you have to optimize your resources. Depending on how well you do this, your business can take various different directions; it can go uphill, or fail, or get lost. The way to determine what is the correct way of using the available time and cash is by having a clear understanding of the goals you have set out to accomplish. It isn't enough to say you want to succeed; you must stop and ask yourself what exactly it is that you mean by succeeding.

So let's start by getting the textbook definition of a business and then start going from there. In his book, *The Economist: Guide to Financial Management*, John Tennent says the following: "A business is a commercial operation that provides products or services with the aim of making a profit for the benefit of its owners." This should mean that so long as owners benefitted from their investment, a business can be considered successful. Of course, the question of who the owners actually are will vary from one case to another. Yet another question will come down to whether the desired benefit has to be immediate or in the long term.

Return on Investment

When you are deciding if you prefer to apply an immediate strategy or a more long-lasting one, you need to first come up with a method of measuring progress. In managerial accounting, this is known as the return on investment. Return on Investment (ROI) is a concept intended to give an algebraic solution to the questions: Did business generate a profit? And how much was it? These are important questions, and you can't rely on personal impressions to answer them, so the way of determining the ROI is actually an equation.

$$ROI = \frac{Profit}{Investment}\%$$

For example, if you invest $2000 in your business this year, and the net profit you generated is around $500, to determine this year's ROI all you have to do is divide 500 by 2000, which gives a resulting figure of 0.25, that is to say, 25%. Your business's ROI for this year, therefore, would be 25%, which is not bad at all.

There isn't a straightforward way to calculate ROI on QuickBooks simply because, as you might imagine, it is a more abstract ratio. You would first need to tell QBD what specific profit and investment figures to take under consideration, but QBD provides the data for calculating ROI, and it does it in a much faster and error-free manner. And once this is done, the next step is to use this information as the foundation for future decision-making. Typically, the aim should be to reach a healthy ROI percentage over a sustained period. This is done by adopting a strategy that responds to real situations that don't just implement the same plan over and over but rather adapts to what goes on.

The beneficiaries of a business's return on investment are the investors. They will be interested to know how sustainable an ROI your business can deliver and what that average ROI percentage is. You, the person who operates QBD and keeps the books in order, can propose a business strategy that will go along the lines of distribution or reinvestment. A distribution, as the name suggests, means that returns get distributed among investors for them to use outside of business and as they please. On the other hand, a reinvestment means that returns are retained in the business to be used for further growth.

Distributions or reinvestments are management directions that need to be argued for and against, always with one clear goal in mind: to make a significant, consistent, and long-lasting profit for the owners. This normally means applying one of the following business strategy templates:

- For young businesses: giving up early profits and reinvesting heavily to cover operating costs and accomplish growth and expansion.

- For mature businesses: giving up a portion of profits and reinvesting in research or innovation to surpass the competition and secure future profits.

Types of Ownership

Therefore it becomes clear that business owners are at the center of the entire decision-making process, or so it would seem. The case is not the same for every business, as you will see. Management and ownership can be more or less together depending primarily on the size of a business, which can be summed up in these five main types:

- Sole Proprietor

- Partnership

- Limited Liability Partnership (LLP)

- Private Company

- Public Company

If you own everything and are the only one in charge of decision-making, this means you run a Sole Proprietor type of business. If you share these responsibilities with other people, all of you combined to run a Partnership type of business. On the other hand, if you gather investment from private agreements with investors, and maybe you yourself are one of them, that means you run a Private Company type of business. A Limited Liability Partnership would be somewhere between a traditional Partnership and a Private Company. Lastly, when you eventually have an Initial Public Opening (IPO), which means getting a business listed in the stock market for everybody to be able to invest in it, then you run a Public Company type of business, also known as a publicly-traded company.

The criterion for this classification resides in the way in which each business gathers capital to grow. Bigger businesses need more capital, the kind that very few people can amass on their own, so they go to investors, hedge funds, venture capitals, all sources of cash that are truly on another league in terms of size. By contrast, smaller businesses need less capital, the kind that a sole proprietor might be able to contribute on their own, together with other co-proprietors, or with the help of a bank loan.

The more a business grows, the more convenient it is to set owners and managers apart and really draw the shape of a triangle between investment, business and accounting. Like this:

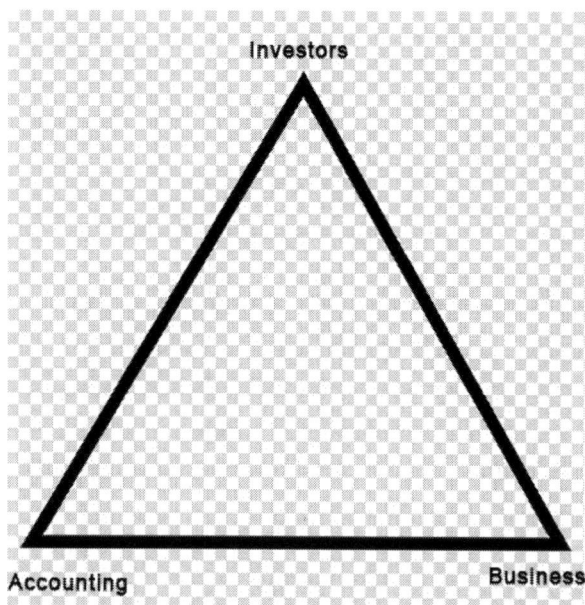

But when you run a small to mid-size business, chances are that these three categories are going to be a bit more mingled. That doesn't mean that business is an entirely different thing now, just that decision-making is more centralized. For instance, suppose you run an ice cream store, and you're both the boss and the employee. In such cases, keep in mind that whatever the size, the general principles remain the same and are to be followed in the same order: Investment/ownership provides cash funds for the business to operate, the business, in turn, uses this cash to make a product and sell it, then accounting supervises all business activities to deliver a briefing on the current status and future prospects.

How to Read a Report

Of course, sooner rather than later, a business is expected to be able to dispense investment and generate cash funds on its own. That is precisely the moment when it becomes pertinent to talk about an actual return on investment. This figure is always going to be a variable, but the entire goal of conducting business is to make it as high and sustainable as possible. And this goal is all the more feasible so long as accounting records are kept neatly, and reports are interpreted correctly. This may well have been repeated various times by now, but that's okay. Tidy records and intelligent report reading are the very mantras of good business management.

You may remember from Chapter Four that there are three main reports, the ones that are required by government authorities and the ones that accounting practice typically regards as its foundation. So let's have a look at how to read a report using those three main reports as an example.

- The Income (or Profit & Loss) Statement

Total income, total expenses, and net income. That is the information every income statement provides. As part of the jargon, total income will always go at the top line of the spreadsheet, which is why it is normally called "the top line", and net income will always go at the bottom, so it's normally called "the bottom line". Big companies add a lot of other additional details than small businesses, but the overall core information and the top and bottom line are all the same.

As I said, an income statement assesses business performance over a set period, and the way it does this is by contrasting what you've earned with what you've spent, thereby determining which of those two figures was bigger. Because of its relation with time, many will say the income statement is a way of telling a story. Here's how you have to read that story.

The main thing in an income statement is to have a comparison parameter. You don't want to look at a single year's report; you want to have several years side by side and compare. When doing this, you basically have to look for a sign of good health, which is located at the progressive changes in total income and net income. Total income represents the amount of money that a business has generated without yet putting into account the expenses that were incurred in the process. Net income represents the amount of money that the business was actually able to earn after expenses have been taken out.

Over the course of income statements from several years, a decreasing net income figure would be bad news even if the total income figure increased. Furthermore, a situation like this could suggest that production has grown, but not in an efficient way. But not to worry. A natural reaction to solve the problem would be to revise the production chain in search of inefficiencies so that you can rethink and change them. If this was done successfully, then next year's income statement should yield a higher net income figure, even if total income were to stay exactly the same.

Healthy progress over the course of various years' income statements would show up in the form of increases both in total income and net income. This would mean that after the costs of the goods sold, after depreciation, and all other additional costs, a business was still capable of generating revenue—an amount of cash that is not tied to any liability and can be destined to distribution or reinvestment.

- The Balance Sheet

Assets, liabilities, and equity. Those are the three elements a balance sheet is expected to report. The way in which these have to be related is, once again, set by the accounting equation.

Assets = Liabilities + Equity

This was shown back in Chapter One, but to explain it in a new way, think of it as two roads that are expected to lead to exactly the same place. If they didn't, then you'd be in trouble. Remember: double-entry bookkeeping means correlating a side of credits and a side of debits, with equity being a plug figure to tell you what you own, but also to hold the equation stable. So you can actually arrange the equation differently in order to calculate equity.

Equity = Assets - Liabilities

Let's go through this last part once more, just in case. As you know, all transactions are either inflows or outflows. Since the balance sheet doesn't show the behavior of transactions over time but rather at a single moment, its aim is not to show what took place in the past, but rather how everything is right now and what is supposed to happen next. So the goal is to know what you have (assets) and what you will have to pay back (liabilities), but knowing all along that, depending on whether you have more than what you owe or vice versa, these two amounts are not going to be equal.

This is where equity comes in. First of all, it's a way to let you enter all inflows that have been recorded as direct owner's contributions. Second, even in the absence of any contributions, equity will always be the resulting amount of the difference between what you have and what you owe. If equity has a negative value, then your debts surpass your assets. If it has a positive value, then your assets surpass your debts.

The balance sheet will be arranged in two halves, one for assets and another for liabilities and equity. The reason it's called a balance sheet is that having equity as the plug figure to keep the equation stable, now these two halves have to be balanced. Each has to deliver the same resulting amount. Another distinction to note is that all three categories will include a section for current and non-current items. The reason for this last part is that the report needs to make it clear which items are due to change in the next twelve months (current ones) and which are due to change later in time (non-current ones).

When looking at a balance sheet, you want to look for signs of an increase in equity that is not explained by owners' or investors' contributions. For instance, a common critique thrown at venture capitals nowadays is that they can lure you into thinking that business is going well but are actually just huge amounts of equity that can disguise the rest of the equation. It's the same as saying that you're looking for proof of business profitability, not just sheer cash availability. If a business can increase equity over the long term, and every balance sheet it delivers reflects that, then it will do very well as an investment.

- The Statement of Cash Flow

The three areas shown in this report are the operating, investing, and financing cash flows, which respectively refer to the costs of keeping business open, the expenses for further growth, and the debt that is acquired to compensate for any of the previous two. A cash flow statement is frequently confused as being a direct reflection of profit. It isn't. It simply tells you how much cash has passed through your business over time, either in the form of income, expense, or debt acquisition.

There is also a direct and an indirect method of making a statement of cash flow, which depends on whether you're employing the cash or the accrual method of bookkeeping. Given that QuickBooks operates under the accrual method by default, and also given that this is probably going to be your preferred or mandated method anyway, you have to keep in mind what this implies in a statement of cash flow. It basically means that cash flows are not necessarily recorded at the precise moment when cash is exchanged but rather whenever a transaction takes place. For instance, if you have programmed expenses every month, but sometimes you pay for some of these in advance. Contrary to what you might think, this does not mean that you can record one single transaction for the months you paid in advance. Under the accrual method, transactions get recorded independently of the actual cash exchange.

When reading a statement of cash flow, what you're essentially looking for are signs of liquidity. This is important when you're interested in determining future actions but want to do so in an informed manner. For instance, if you're planning on expanding business, maybe opening up a new branch, purchasing inventory stock, or something similar, but you're not sure if it is the right time in terms of financial health, the cash flow statement is the report you want to check. It will show you exactly how much money goes through your business, and it will organize it in the three areas that I mentioned: an operating cash flow to show you how much cash was destined to cover operational costs, an investing cash flow to show you how much has been spent on further growth (if anything), and a financing cash flow to show you how much has been taken as loans and will have to be paid back.

You can also look for signs of loss compensation, and these are indeed worrisome signs. What happens is that the investing and financing cash flows can have negative values without too much problem, but the same cannot happen to the operating cash flow under any circumstance. Of course, it can happen, but when it does, it means that you're truly spending more than what you earn. If you need to compensate, what will naturally happen next is you will reach out for some kind of loan, and this will solve things for a short time. However, it will only make the situation worse because now you'll owe even more cash, and your financial situation won't necessarily have improved. Yes, this sounds terrible, but it's better to read about it, to be aware of this risk than to experience it yourself.

Meanwhile, investing and financing cash flows can have negative values without putting the business in an emergency. So why is that? The thing is that when a business is growing, it needs to fund different activities that represent a cost. But even the business feels its weight; it is still too soon to decide whether it's a bad expense or a good expense because, above all, it's an investment. Whatever it may accomplish for business performance remains to be seen. That being said, you want to avoid being immediately positive about negative investing cash flows. They can be both good and bad, not just one of the two.

Financing cash flows are closely related to this because they represent loans, that is to say, future liabilities. It could be said that when you happen to find too high a value in the financing cash flow, you can interpret this in one of two ways depending on the value of the other two cash flows. If, in addition to a high financing cash flow you also have a negative operating cash flow, then there are no two ways around it: the business is in serious trouble and things really need to straighten up to avoid bankruptcy. On the other hand, if the other high cash flow is not operating, but instead the investing cash flow, then it probably means that business is expanding and the way it's doing it is not by its own funds, but rather through outside sources. And again, this last option is not immediately good nor bad.

How to Do More With Less

A normal concern for those who can grasp financial reports and spend a good amount of time interpreting them is the question: Which sign should I pay attention to first? In other words, how to set priorities after the assessment process. In many cases, this will come down to what looks more urgent, and so it won't be so difficult. But the rest of the time, it will be about getting relatively uniform signs and identifying those with the potential to be transcendental. In accountancy, this last case scenario is addressed by something called the 80-20 rule, which is formulated as follows: In any situation, 80% of the consequences will be a result of 20% of all causes.

Also known as the Pareto Principle, the so-called 80-20 rule tells you that most consequences are a result of a small portion of all causes. In other words, the most transcendental events come out of tiny, seemingly trivial things. Once you start taking this rule seriously and giving it a central spot in your list of concerns, the natural conclusion will be the question: How can I identify those tiny crucial causes that will lead to big consequences? And how can I know if those consequences mean good or bad news for business?

One of the answers is to think about the weather, so to speak. Let's look at this with an example. If you buy computer pieces to assemble them and sell them again ready for use, it will interest you to know that a recent spike in the GPU world market has occurred because crypto miners found out GPUs are useful to them. As a result of this completely unrelated eventuality, there is a global decrease in the availability of GPUs, and this causes it to cost almost double the original price. Your profit margin will be affected because you'll need to spend more on raw materials. If you try to compensate for this by increasing the retail price, this could also affect your sales rate. It's a small thing, one of the many pieces you need to assemble computers, but the effect it can have on the entire chain is not at all insignificant. And this has to do with one simple trading truth: everybody's profit is someone else's loss. Value doesn't just get increased or managed. Above all, it fluctuates, affecting every business in a range of different ways.

Another way of appreciating the validity of the 80-20 rule could be to look back at QuickBooks reports. In business, there are always going to be lots of different factors at play, and recognizing those that are fundamental will not always be easy or even possible, but the important thing is that you don't take guesses anymore when you can read the reports and pay attention to what they tell you. Once you have a sense of the state of every aspect of your business, go back and think about the 80-20 rule again and see if it still seems vague.

Accounting with QuickBooks

Two of the most intimidating things in QuickBooks, in the beginning, can be the sheer amount of settings that you have to go through and the difficulty in finding reports useful. The way to try and fix the first problem is by embedding the settings for new customers, items, forms, etc., into the transaction recording process as well. In spite of that, you can think of it this way: The more careful you are at setting good templates and presets at the beginning, the more automatic everything will be the rest of the time.

If QuickBooks does ask you tons of things at first, it is because it wants to remember your information appropriately, so you don't have to fill it out later manually. It's a bit challenging at first but then becomes smooth.

About the second problem, you now have an explanation of how you're supposed to interpret the three main accounting reports. But the cliche is true: Every single business is indeed different. Many universal rules are going to remain applicable, and this is what QuickBooks is designed to help with, but down the road, you'll have to get to know your own business, how it behaves, how it changes with time, how it tells you what it needs and what it doesn't need. According to this, you're gradually going to learn how to customize a report specific to your needs, but above all, you'll learn the importance of keeping a record of everything. The only way in which QuickBooks will not be useful to you is if you're not consistent with the most humble but crucial of all accounting activities: every day's bookkeeping entries.

Other than that, once again, you can always get a test drive by clicking on the Open Sample File button when you first run QuickBooks. Let's face it, opening your first company file on QuickBooks is not as mundane as creating a Facebook account. You can't afford to press the wrong buttons on QuickBooks. It's always a good idea to familiarize yourself with the software before putting your own information there.

Another thing you can do before you start is to look at some real-life reports. For example, you can go check *Yahoo Finance*, which offers free financial information from real publicly traded companies. Once you're on the website, type in the name of whatever company you want, like Apple or Amazon, and then go to the Financials tab. There you will find all three major reports with real, live information that gets updated all the time. Take your time to study them and even compare them with your own reports. Of course, many details will not look exactly the same, but the general format and structure are bound to follow the same rules.

Main Takeaways

- Return on Investment is a percentage that shows business performance based on the data provided by QuickBooks reports. It is useful for managers such as yourself, as well as investors.

- There are five types of businesses according to who are their owners: Sole proprietorships, Partnerships, Limited Liability Partnerships (LLP), Private Companies, and Public Companies. QuickBooks is primarily aimed at any of the first three types.

- Learning how to interpret reports will enable you to distinguish significant data from irrelevant data, which in turn will let you establish wiser priorities.

In the next chapter, you will...

- Get a list of valuable tips for QuickBooks users.

- Get a list of things to stay away from.

- Get a brief explanation of some integrations that are available for QuickBooks Desktop.

CHAPTER EIGHT

ADVANCED TIPS, INTEGRATIONS AND COMMON MISTAKES TO AVOID

In this chapter, you will get a reference list of some of the tips and know-hows that an experienced QuickBooks user should have, and then a list of some common mistakes to avoid. Also, even though QBO is the one that's designed to operate with third-party integrations, at the end, there will be a section dedicated to some integrations available for QBD that you might find useful. So let's just dive right into it.

Advanced Tips

- Positioning the Icon Bar

As I said, in QuickBooks, there are two additional bars surrounding the home page: the toolbar up above and the icon bar on the left side. The latter is movable; you can switch it from the left side to the top and vice versa. Do this by following these steps:

View > Top Icon Bar

Or alternatively:

View > Left Icon Bar

- Using Colors in the Chart of Accounts

When you have used QuickBooks for a significant amount of time, it's possible that your chart of accounts might get cluttered with too many accounts and subaccounts. This could make it hard for you to distinguish one thing from the other. In that case, QuickBooks offers you the possibility to choose colors for different groups, so you can just glance at your chart of accounts and still know what you're looking at. To do this, go to:

Edit > Preferences > Desktop View > Switch to Colored Icons

- Knowing When to Use Invoices and Sales Receipts

This was already explained in Chapter Five, but it doesn't hurt to say it once more, just in case. Both invoices and sales receipts are forms used to record income transactions. Invoices are for recording income where the payment will arrive later, whereas sales receipts are for recording income from immediate payments. So, the basic advice is this:

Only use invoices for customers who pay over time, and only use sales receipts for customers who pay beforehand.

- Using the Migration Tool

Intuit's migration tool is designed to help you transfer your license and company file into another computer, provided that you're using QuickBooks 2018 or any of the following versions. In order to work properly, it requires you to take a couple of previous, rather obvious, measures. First, you need to create a backup of your company file by following these steps:

File > Backup Company > Create Local Backup

The second thing is to go and install the same version of QBD on the new computer you intend to use. After this, you can proceed with the actual migration process.

File > Utilities > Move QuickBooks to another computer

The program will prompt you to create a new password. Do not confuse it with your everyday password. This one is just to secure the migration. Choose a storage destination, some flash drive unit where you can save and move the file, and you're done. Go to the new computer, and inside your flash drive, look for a file called Move_QuickBooks.bat. Click on it, type in the password you just created, and the migration tool will do the rest. The process can take minutes or hours, depending on your hardware and the size of the file you're migrating.

- Updating QuickBooks Desktop

One of the main differences between QBD and QBO, as I said at the beginning, is that QBO is constantly and automatically updated, whereas you need to manually update QBD every year. This is how you can do the latter.

Help > Update QuickBooks Desktop

This will take you to a window with three tabs, and there, you'll find that it is possible to automate updates even in QBD. The first tab, Overview, shows whether automatic updates are enabled and also the option to update manually. The second tab, Options, shows what updates are available and the option to toggle automatic updates on or off. In this second tab, you'll also find an option to toggle shared downloads on and off. This is to share updates with other computers when you have a company file accessible from various computers. The third and last tab, Update Now, shows a history of all previous updates.

When updating, keep in mind that this process can only take place with an internet connection. Also, that updated features will not come into effect until you restart the program.

- Setting Up Multi-User Network

Having a multi-user network means that one single company file is accessible from more than one computer but with pre-established restrictions for each one. In a situation like this, the company file is stored on the main computer, called the server, and other computers, called workstations, also have access to it but don't actually have it saved on their memories. This is useful, for example, when you need an easy way of sharing accounting information with your staff but don't wish to give full admin privileges.

First, install QBD on the server computer choosing the Custom and Network Install option. This will bring up two alternatives to assign a different type of installation for the server computer and for the workstations. For the server computer, choose the option to confirm that you'll both be using and hosting your company file on that computer. For the workstations, choose the option to confirm that you'll only be using the company file. Set differentiated permissions for each computer by downloading and installing QuickBooks Tool Hub. Then, run this program and follow these steps:

Company File Issues > Run QuickBooks File Doctor

This will check that everything is correctly set for multi-user access and tell you what to do in case of errors. The next step is to check the boxes for all the things that you want each computer to have access to. Follow these steps to do that:

Properties > Security > Advanced > QBData Service User

This will bring up a list of actions for you to click on the Allowed option every time you wish to allow the computer to do that specific action. After doing this for every computer on the network, you have to download and install QuickBooks Database Server Manager on the server computer, but you have to do this from the QuickBooks program. Like this:

File > Switch to multi-user mode > Yes

Now the multi-user network is set up. The server manager will run in the background, even when the server computer is off, to monitor other workstations. You can set new users for every workstation by following these steps:

Company > Users > Setup Users and Roles > New

- Transferring from QuickBooks Desktop to QuickBooks Online

If you're interested in doing this, keep in mind that there is no turning back and that the product you will now have, though it's the same, has an overall different design philosophy. This was amply explained in Chapter Two, but basically, QBO relies much more on integrations and customizations than QBD does.

First of all, if you haven't already, make sure that you have the latest QBD update installed. Also, check the number of targets that your company file has. If it exceeds 350,000, then you need to compress your file, and some current targets might need to be archived to reduce space. Check the number of targets by opening the Product Information window (by pressing F2 for Windows or CMD + 1 for Mac).

The last and most important preventive measure is to backup your company file, which you can do either by using the Migration Tool or simply copying and pasting the file to a different memory drive. This won't really have any further use; it's just in case of errors.

Start transferring your file by following these steps:

Company > Export Company File to QuickBooks Online

A window will appear where you can choose to start moving your company file right away or begin a QBO trial period. This is because you can do the process both before or after having set a new QBO subscription. You'll be asked if you prefer to create a new account or sign in with the one you already have. Simply click the options you prefer and follow the instructions. Since Intuit will use the information from your existing company file, you won't need to enter too much else, just some basic information, like your name and address.

Your current QBD subscription and company name will then be shown. If you wish, you can change the name, and naturally, the subscription will stay there because now you'll switch to a QBO subscription instead. For this, though, keep in mind that only the QBO Plus and QBO Advanced plans come with inventory tracking tools, in case that's something you need. Click on Continue, then on Upload, and you're done.

The upload will take somewhere between minutes and hours, depending on your hardware, your bandwidth, and the size of your file. When it's finished, you'll get an email to confirm it. Before using QBO, make sure to run a couple of reports from both versions, always using the same date ranges, to compare them and see if everything's in order.

Common Mistakes to Avoid

- QuickBooks Desktop's System Requirements

QBD is available both for Windows and Macintosh, but the most comprehensive alternative is the Windows version. Furthermore, the two versions are not 100%

compatible with each other, so switching back and forth will produce some errors and undesired changes. It would be ideal to opt for one and stay with it until the end.

On the hardware side, you'll be fine with any 2.4 GHz processor, but if possible do go for something stronger since it will help with performance, especially when conducting tough computing operations. A 4 to 8 GB RAM memory is recommended. For file storage, the recommendation is an average of 3 GB, preferably on an SSD instead of a regular hard drive. The visual display will be all the more comfortable with more than one screen, but the high resolution is not a must. The idea is you're not trying to watch 4K videos, but just to see various reports and graphs all at once.

- Keeping Separate Accounts

This is mainly procedural advice. It is good practice to create separate accounts for each bank account that you want to link to QuickBooks. If you link various QBD accounts to the same bank account, what will happen is you'll lose the ability to visualize how different funds end up in different places. It's better to keep both QuickBooks and real-life accounts in sync with each other.

- Making Deposits

As you know, the last stage in the bookkeeping process with QuickBooks is located at the Banking Center, where you actually make the deposits. However, having gone through this step doesn't yet mean that the money now sits in your bank account. There is an additional step for this, one that regrettably takes place outside of QuickBooks.

First, combine all the payments you wish to put together and send them to the Undeposited Funds account, the one where all income transactions are supposed to go before they've been assigned a destination. This is just in case you haven't already put them there. Next, go ahead and make the bank deposit, either physically or electronically. Make sure to keep your deposit slip. Then go back to QBD and click on the Make Deposits icon. Re-select all the deposits you wish to combine, then click OK, and from the pop-up window, select the account you want to send them to. Check the combined total and make sure that it coincides with the amount indicated on your deposit slip. Enter the date you made the deposit, and then click on Save & Close.

- Enabling Multiple Currencies

If you want to enable the multiple currencies option on QuickBooks, you can go to:

Edit > Preferences > Multiple Currencies > Company Preferences

From there, click on the button that says "Yes, I use more than one currency" and select the one you prefer to set as your home currency.

When doing this, keep in mind that enabling multiple currencies alters your balance and that this is an irreversible process. What you want to do is back up your company file before enabling the option so you can go back in case of errors.

Also, keep in mind that online banking and payroll are only available when your home currency is set to USD.

- Deleting Transactions

Sometimes you will want to delete a transaction because of a mistake, an annulment, or other reason. It's important that you avoid doing this at all costs, and if you absolutely must, then consult with an accountant beforehand. What happens is that QuickBooks has many transactions linked to one another, so if you inadvertently or intentionally delete one of them, you might be affecting several others in the background without even noticing it.

Anyway, once you decide to do it, there are two options. One is to "void" a transaction, and the other is to actually delete it. Both options can be accessed via the same path. Just go to the transaction in question and follow these steps:

More > Delete > Yes

Or alternatively:

More > Void > Yes

If you choose to void a transaction that has already been paid for, then you'll have to assign which other transaction you want to transfer those payments to. If it's empty, then it will quite simply be disabled and sit there without affecting any related balance anymore. On the other hand, if you choose to delete a transaction, make sure you trace which other ones are linked to it so that no information gets lost or corrupted in the process. And again, it's better not to do it without asking an accountant's advice first.

- Closing Periods

As time goes by, quarterly and annual reports will have to be archived and put in storage. It is good practice to put the archived data under some kind of security measure so that other people can't go back and alter it accidentally. Do this by following these steps:

Edit > Preferences > Accounting

From that window, click on the Company Preferences button, and there you'll see the option to set passwords for any specific date range. Just choose whichever you prefer and keep that information private so that in the future, only you, the admin user, can access the oldest data.

Third-Party Integrations for QBD

- QODBC

This stands for QuickBooks Open Database Connectivity, and if you haven't had enough acronyms yet, this is indeed a helpful tool that comes free with QuickBooks Desktop Enterprise subscriptions. Its purpose is to make QuickBooks' data more friendly with other external applications through a universal system known simply as ODBC. This establishes a live link between QuickBooks and another application so that data gets transferred and updated all the time.

First, download and install the QODBC driver on your computer. You'll be prompted to enter your registration key, which you'll already have if you purchased the QBD Enterprise subscription, or you can also choose the 30-day test mode for free. After installation, it's important that you have QuickBooks running to establish the connection. Open your QuickBooks company file, then open the QODBC Setup Screen and click on the Test Connection to QuickBooks button. Test the connection by opening the VB Demo application and following these steps:

Connection > Add a new connection

This will bring out a drop-down menu from where you can choose QuickBooks. After having done this, when the QODBC driver is running, QuickBooks will demand that you authorize access. Click on the Yes, Always button, and you're done. From that point on, you don't even need to have QuickBooks running for other applications to use the ODBC protocol and have a live connection to your accounting data.

- Excel & Word

QuickBooks is compatible with Microsoft Office thanks to the QODBC driver, so it's possible to link data between both platforms. The instructions for this are explained above, so here you will see how to actually take advantage of it.

From Excel or Word, click on the top Data tab to open the drop-down menu and follow these steps:

Data > Get External Data > New Database Query

If this doesn't work, it means you're missing the Microsoft Query Addon, in which case just download the addon and repeat the process. This will bring up a window asking you to pick the source from which you want to pull data into Excel. Select QuickBooks, select the specific lists you want to import, click on the button to view and edit data and click OK. A list of names will appear on the left side. When you click on one of these, a spreadsheet will pull and display the corresponding data directly from QuickBooks. Any changes you make from the accounting software will immediately update on Excel, meaning that this is a live connection.

- Using Excel Pivot Tables

Pivot Tables are a way of quickly deriving specific information from an Excel spreadsheet, but without having to create a new one from scratch. This can be particularly useful to assess reports because it allows you quickly to filter out all undesired data and only look at selected elements. It basically lets you rearrange a spreadsheet from a simple list of filter criteria.

In this case, you'll see how to use pivot tables to navigate your general ledger better. Assuming you have used the QODBC drive, you can pull data directly from Excel. If not, simply go to QuickBooks, run a General Ledger report, and follow these steps:

Reports > Excel > Create New Worksheet > Export

Open the resulting spreadsheet from Excel and proceed to clean it up first. Remove the unnecessary rows and columns, which are all those that appear empty. Below every account row, there will also be a certain number of empty boxes. Copy the account numbers or names from each top box and paste them on the blank ones. Then follow these steps:

Insert > Pivot Table

A new blank spreadsheet with some new options will appear. To the right, there will be a list of fields that you can check or uncheck and move to any of four main categories: filters, columns, rows, and values. Using these tools, you can start filtering the source spreadsheet in different ways according to your choosing.

- Veryfi

This is a bookkeeping application that renders all kinds of physical forms into electronically organized information. It's primarily designed to help you record information when you're on the go. For example, it allows you to take photos and scan them to extract the information and put it in a database. Granted, QBD is more than capable of doing the same thing, but if you happen to use Veryfi and wish to connect it with QBD, it's possible to do it.

Normally what will happen is you'll be interested in switching from Veryfi to QuickBooks, which is a more complex and complete tool. From Veryfi, just go to the listed integrations, click on the QuickBooks Desktop option, click on the Information button and read the instructions to transfer the data. Basically, you will have to export your chart of accounts, customers, vendors, and item lists to generate an .iif that makes them all compatible with QBD.

- InEight

This is a construction project management software. It allows you to make estimates, conduct monitor projects in a cloud-based fashion. If you need accounting software but are also within this specific line of business, then it's a good tool for you, and it can thankfully integrate with QuickBooks.

InEight provides a variety of plugins, one of which enables the option to connect to QBD. This integration allows you to send estimates and jobs from InEight straight into QBD to manage the accounting side of the job from there. You might be interested to know that QBD Enterprise offers customizations for specific lines of business, construction being one of them, so again, even for a construction business, you can keep all activities centralized on QBD if you prefer.

- Reach Reporting

This is a tool to generate advanced reports. It pulls the data from your accounting software and uses it to generate all sorts of customized or template-based reports that illustrate business performance.

Connect with QBD by adding your company from the Reach Reporting interface, choosing the company file you wish to connect, and downloading the Desktop Connector. Then run the downloaded file and log in with your Reach Reporting account information, choose your company file again, and select the sync preferences that suit you best. Now your QBD company file is synced with Reach Reporting, and you'll be able to run reports on either one with the same accounting data.

Main Takeaways

- Deleting transactions is a possibility inside QuickBooks, but it's one that you should think about carefully and avoid most of the time.

- Always back up your company file.

- Migrating from QBO into QBD is a simple but irreversible process.

- Unlike QBO, QBD doesn't excel on third-party integrations, but there are still some good options. Above all, the QODBC protocol makes it compatible with some pretty interesting tools.

FINAL WORDS

To close, it'd be good to go back to the initial question: Have you ever thought about becoming an accountant? And again, this rhetorical question is not trying to make you consider the profession. It's just meant to show you the implications of using any accounting software.

A common mistake that people make is they will get a QuickBooks subscription, pay for it, and then use the software just for when money goes in and out of business. This comes from a typical prejudice that we have about modern technology. We tend to think of it either as something meant for leisure, like Facebook or YouTube, or as something overly complicated and intimidating, like accounting software.

One of the goals of this book was to illustrate how, in reality, no accounting software will magically solve your problems. If you want to get the most out of QuickBooks, it's important that you understand that, and at least familiarize yourself with the basic accounting concepts. Only by doing this can you understand their implications as you go around pressing buttons. Of course, making accountancy less monotonous or basic is not as simple as streaming videos, but if you give QuickBooks a chance, you'll see that it's actually quite intuitive. Once you learn to interpret reports like an expert, it might even become fun!

Manufactured by Amazon.ca
Bolton, ON

22301083R00085